GROWING CLOSE

ACTIVITIES
FOR BUILDING FRIENDSHIPS AND UNITY IN YOUTH GROUPS

Group

Loveland, Colorado

Growing Close
Activities for Building Friendships and Unity in Youth Groups
Copyright ©1996 Group Publishing, Inc.

Credits
Contributing Authors: Katrina Arbuckle, Chip Borgstadt, Rick Bundschuh, Karen Dockrey, Mikal Keefer, Paul Kelly, Janice Long, Darrell Pearson, Siv Ricketts, and Michael D. Warden
Editor: Stephen Parolini
Managing Editor: Paul Woods
Chief Creative Officer: Joani Schultz
Copy Editor: Julie Meiklejohn
Art Director: Helen H. Lannis
Cover Designer: Liz Howe
Computer Graphic Artist: Rosalie Lawrence
Cover Photographer: Craig DeMartino
Illustrator: Tim Foley
Production Manager: Gingar Kunkel

Library of Congress Cataloging-in-Publication Data

Growing close : activities for building friendships and unity in youth groups.
     p.   cm.
   ISBN 1-55945-709-0
     1. Group relations training—Problems, exercises, etc. 2. Group games.
3. Church work with youth—Problems, exercises, etc.
HM134.G76 1996
302'.14—dc20
                                     96-18146
                                       CIP

ISBN 1-55945-709-0

10 9 8 7 6 5 4   05 04 03 02 01 00 99
Printed in the United States of America.

Visit our Web site: www.grouppublishing.com

Contents

identity-Builders

Introduction

admit it. You're getting a little tired of the same old crowdbreakers. Sure, they've served you well in the past. But they just don't grab kids the way they used to. In fact, you're haunted by phrases such as "Didn't we just do this last week?" and "I already know how this turns out." Well, your haunted days are over. This book is packed with 75 new crowdbreakers which will break up the boredom and repetition that may be infecting your otherwise stellar youth group program.

And that's not all . . . this book also includes 75 identity-building activities—the kind that can truly build your kids into a cohesive and supportive community.

We know you want to go straight to the activities, so we won't keep you. Go ahead and skim the book for new ideas to use right away—most of the activities require few or simple supplies, so they're easy to prepare. And all of the activities involve the whole group.

But before you stray too far from this introduction, allow us to define what we mean by crowdbreakers and identity-builders.

Crowdbreakers (also known as icebreakers or mixers) are designed to help kids get to know each other on a very basic, surface level. While some of these activities help kids learn simple information about each other, such as names, interests, and hobbies, all of the activities are designed to get kids moving around and enjoying each other's company. That's all crowdbreakers need to accomplish—because when kids are relaxed and enjoying one another's company, the rest of the meeting is more likely to be successful.

Identity-builders are designed to help your group members grow closer to each other while developing a sense of group identity. Unlike crowdbreakers, identity-builders are designed to go beneath the surface and get kids thinking about the nature of the group and how they contribute to it.

Some of these activities help to forge a specific group identity through a project or the creation of a group symbol. Others, through creative interaction, help kids discover specific roles each group member plays within the group. Use identity-builders often to help strengthen the bonds that make your group a positive force for God.

That's it. We're finished "preaching to the choir." Now flip through these pages, and start breathing new life into your youth group meetings by using these creative crowdbreakers and identity-builders.

Tip: You'll find a few of these "Tips" scattered throughout this book. Read them. They can help you tailor the activities to your youth group's needs. ■

Crowd-breakers

airline High Jinks

preparation: You'll need pencils, scissors, paper clips, a variety of colored paper, and photocopies of the "Paper Helicopter" handout (p. 12) on colored paper.

description: Give kids paper, pencils, scissors, paper clips, and "Paper Helicopter" handouts. Have each person make a paper airplane or helicopter (see handout on page 12). Then have them write their names and one of the following questions (something they wouldn't mind answering) on their aircraft:

- Where have you lived in your life?
- When did you become a Christian?
- What question would you like to ask God?
- What's your favorite thing about this group?

Move your group to a place that is conducive to a good paper-airplane launch (such as a balcony or the end of a large room). Have kids "launch" their planes or helicopters. Then have each person retrieve someone else's aircraft, find the person named on it, and ask that person the question written on the plane or helicopter.

Gather everyone in a circle, and have kids introduce their partners and tell what they learned about them.

Tip: *Encourage kids to take their partners' planes or helicopters home as a reminder to pray for their new friends during the coming week.* ■

Paper Helicopter

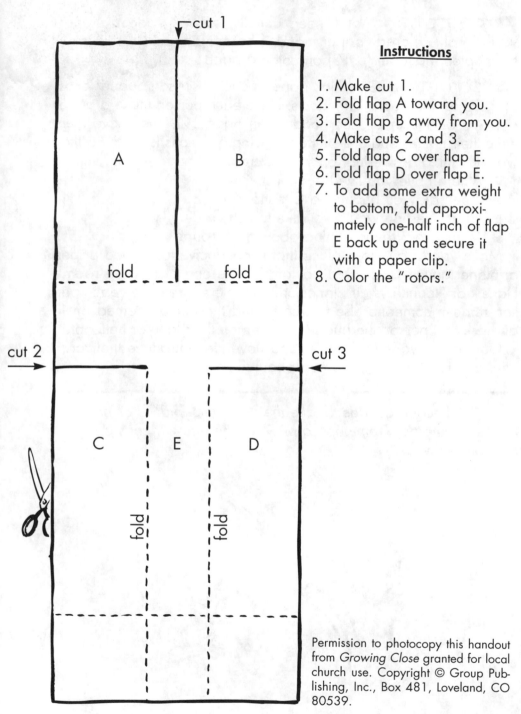

Instructions

1. Make cut 1.
2. Fold flap A toward you.
3. Fold flap B away from you.
4. Make cuts 2 and 3.
5. Fold flap C over flap E.
6. Fold flap D over flap E.
7. To add some extra weight to bottom, fold approximately one-half inch of flap E back up and secure it with a paper clip.
8. Color the "rotors."

alpha Ralpha Zot

preparation: For this activity you'll need to select two energetic, outgoing co-conspirators from your group. Before the meeting, instruct them to devise a secret handshake and to learn it well enough to teach it to the other members of your group. The key is for them to develop an involved, complicated handshake that can be learned in about two minutes.

description: After kids have gathered, say: **Congratulations! You've all been selected for membership in Alpha Ralpha Zot, the most prestigious fraternity of them all! You're pre-approved, ready to go, with just one tiny hurdle left to clear—you've all got to learn the official Alpha Ralpha Zot secret handshake.**

Fortunately, two ARZ members are here to demonstrate the handshake for you. Stand up, and let our ARZ members teach you the handshake that will forever after help you to recognize a fellow member of Alpha Ralpha Zot.

After your group has learned and practiced the handshake, form three groups, and have kids discuss the following questions:

■ **How did it feel to be inducted into ARZ?**

■ **What did it feel like to learn the secret handshake?**

■ **How do we recognize others as Christians when we meet them?**

■ **Why is it sometimes difficult to identify other people as Christians?**

Read John 13:34-35 aloud, then form pairs, and have partners create their own greetings (a handshake or another signal) that illustrates one aspect of the Christian faith. For example, a pair might create a greeting that includes making the sign of the cross.

Have kids mingle and offer their greetings to each other.

amusing Amusements

preparation: You'll need newsprint and a marker.

description: Have kids nominate their favorite amusement park rides. List the top five on a sheet of newsprint, then have kids vote to choose the group favorite. Have kids work together to create a facsimile of this ride, using only themselves and items in the room. For example, kids might create a roller coaster by forming a circle and adjusting the heights of their heads to indicate the varying heights of the roller coaster track. To complete this ride, kids might grab a volleyball and move it around the "track" with their hands (see illustration). Encourage kids to be creative and to involve everyone in the activity. If your group has more than 20 kids, form multiple groups of 10 to 20 kids each, and let each group create a different ride.

If kids want a real challenge, suggest one of the following rides: a Ferris wheel, a "tram" ride (the kind that travels at a great height over the park, like a ski lift), or a log-flume ride.

answering-Machine Scavenger Hunt

preparation: You'll need about 10 working answering machines. Ask church members who will let you use their machines to help out by recording clues on their machines on the day of the event and allowing the machines to answer any calls during the event.

description: Let answering machines give the clues for your next scavenger hunt. Arrange which clue will be in each greeting and in which order kids are to call the numbers. Use the first phone number as an announcement telling kids where to meet to begin the event. It may work best for the first number to be a church number. The first greeting might be "Tonight's meeting begins with an answering-machine scavenger hunt, beginning at the church at 6:30. It will end around 8:30. Bring a notepad, a pen or pencil, and a dollar to help purchase scavenger hunt items your group can't otherwise acquire."

When teenagers arrive at the starting location, form teams of four. Provide an adult driver for each team, and give each driver the second phone number. Then have teams head out to find a phone on which to dial the number. On that machine kids might hear a clue such as "Find something green. Then go to Gary's house, and find the phone number taped to his back door. Dial that number to hear your next clue."

When kids find that note and dial the number, the next clue might be "Go to a grocery store for a bag of microwave popcorn. Dial the number in which the last four digits spell CORN and the first three digits are the same as the first three digits in the church's phone number." (Adapt this for the number you use, of course).

Add scavenger hunt clues and items appropriate to your location. With the final clue, lead kids to a final meeting place. This crowdbreaker works especially well for a meeting about communication or discussing clues to understanding God's love.

Tip: *Have kids collect things that will ultimately play a part in your meeting, such as items for an activity or snacks for a party. If you don't have time for 10 clues, shorten the scavenger hunt as necessary.* ■

baked Potatoes

preparation: You'll need green and yellow paper and several rolls of aluminum foil. You'll also need a silly, potato-related prize.

description: Form teams of four, and give each team green paper, yellow paper, and a roll of aluminum foil. Have each team choose one member to be a "spudmeister." On "go" have teams race to transform their spudmeisters into human baked potatoes, using the supplies you've provided as well as any others they can find. Tell teams that the first team to finish will win a prize.

Once teams finish, award a prize to the team that finished first. Examples of fun prizes are a sack of potatoes and a large order of French fries. You can also award prizes for the Most Beautiful Potato, the Lumpiest Potato, and the Most Creative Use of Aluminum Foil.

For fun take instant-print pictures of the teams' "spud" works, and display them on a wall.

barrier Busters

preparation: You'll need newspapers, masking tape, and various silly awards.

description: Set out newspapers and tape. Have kids form pairs, and say: **When I say "go," your task will be to create a free-standing physical barrier between yourself and your partner that keeps you from seeing each other. You can use any materials here in the room, including the supplies I've provided. Ready? Go!**

Once pairs have completed their barriers, give awards in various categories, such as the Thickest Barrier, the Weirdest Barrier, or the Most Creative Use of Newspaper. After you've given awards, have pairs race to destroy their barriers. Then say:

Building barriers can be fun, but not nearly as much fun as tearing them down. In this group, we're committed to tearing down barriers between each other. So let's get to it!

blindfolded Bumper-Bodies

preparation: You'll need blindfolds.

description: Have adult sponsors assist you in blindfolding each person. Have kids fold their arms across their chests while you and the other sponsors spin them around three times to disorient them. Tell blindfolded teenagers not to move until you give the signal.

When everyone is successfully disoriented, turn off the lights, and tell kids to carefully walk around (with their blindfolds still in place and their arms still folded across their chests) until they bump into or touch someone else. When teenagers bump into someone, they must stop and find out the other person's name and one thing he or she likes to do. Then they may move around again until they bump into another person. Have kids repeat this until each person has bumped into six different people (adjust this number depending on your group size). If kids bump into another person more than once, they must uncover a new bit of information about him or her each time.

Tip: *Encourage kids to use their fingers to keep track of the number of people they've bumped into.* ∎

blindfolded Racers

preparation: You'll need wheelchairs, chairs on wheels, skateboards, or any other items kids can sit on as they're pushed around a room. You'll also need blindfolds, scrap paper, buckets, and markers. You'll want to set up this crowdbreaker in a large room with a floor that won't be marred by the rolling wheels.

description: Form teams of no more than 10, set up simple courses for teams to navigate. The courses should take kids to the opposite end of the room then back again to the starting place. Place a bucket at the halfway point of each course (see illustration).

Have teams line up at the starting line. Give each team one of the wheeled items. Give teams scrap paper and markers, and say: **When I say "go," the person in the front of each line must put on a blindfold then quickly think of something in his or her life he or she could do without. A teammate must then write it on the paper, crumple the paper up, hand it back to the blindfolded person, and push that person around the course.**

As the rider and the pusher get close to the bucket, teammates may call out directions in order to help the blindfolded rider successfully toss the paper into the bucket. Whether or not the rider makes the basket, continue on until you reach the starting place, then repeat the activity with a new rider and a new pusher.

Use this activity as a relay race, with each person riding at least once and pushing at least once. Make sure each pusher writes legibly when writing down the rider's thoughts.

At the end of the activity, the team that made the most baskets can "do without" cleaning up the papers that missed the buckets as the losing team cleans up the area.

Tip: *This crowdbreaker is a great lead-in to a meeting about forgiveness or one discussing ways of living more simply.* ■

broom Balance

preparation: You'll need several brooms.

description: Form groups of no more than four, and give each group a broom. Have each group form a circle and choose a person to go first. Have that person stand in the center of the circle. That person will place the end of the broom handle in his or her open palm and balance the broom as long as possible. While that person is balancing the broom, a different member of each group must tell the whole group how he or she keeps life in balance. When the broom falls (or after one minute), have someone else in the group balance the broom while a different group member shares. Continue until each person has balanced the broom at least once and all group members have shared at least a little bit about keeping life in balance.

Then have kids report some of their groups' insights to the whole group.

Tip: *This crowdbreaker is a great lead-in to a meeting about keeping a balanced perspective on life.* ■

Candy-Color Connections

preparation: You'll need a source of upbeat music, candy that comes in a variety of colors (such as Starburst candy), and a fun prize.

description: Select four different colors of candy, and give each person one candy, making sure to distribute equal numbers of each color. Each color will designate a team. For smaller groups use two colors to create two teams. Have kids form teams according to the candy colors, then let them eat their candy.

Explain that you'll be giving each team a task to accomplish and all teams will be competing to complete their tasks first. The team that completes its task first wins a point for that round, and the team that accumulates the most points by the end of the activity wins the game. Play upbeat music while teams are working. Assign one of the following tasks to all the teams:

Have kids line up according to . . .
- birth month (beginning with January),
- initial of first name (alphabetically),
- number of buttons on clothing (fewest to most),
- initial of last name (alphabetically),
- hair length (shortest to longest),
- number of letters in first name (fewest to most), or
- telephone number (in numerical order).

Assign teams different tasks from the list for subsequent rounds, and continue as long as you'd like.

Award a fun prize to the winning team.

Candy Guess

preparation: You'll need a variety of candies.

description: Form pairs. Have one person in each pair be the Feeder, and the other be the Taster. (Verify that no one is allergic to chocolate or nuts before allowing anyone to feed either of these to a Taster.) Have the Tasters close their eyes, and have the Feeders put candy samples in the Tasters' mouths. See how many Tasters can name the candy correctly. Award bonus points to Tasters who can name the flavor or color of the candy (when applicable). After each sample have kids switch roles and repeat the activity with a different type of candy. Do this until each person has sampled at least three different kinds of candy. Award candy prizes to kids who guessed accurately the most times.

Chain Race

preparation: No preparation is needed for this activity.

description: Form teams of six or fewer, and say: **When I say "go," create the longest chain you can, using only items you brought with you into the room. You can use shoes, jackets, watches, anything within reason—as long as the chain can be lifted from end to end without falling apart. Ready? Go!**

Give teams about three minutes to complete their chains. Once you've tested the chains for sturdiness, compare their lengths, and declare the winner. After a round of applause for the winning team, have kids discuss these questions with their teammates:

■ **What makes a chain strong?**
■ **How is a chain similar to a group of friends?**
■ **How was creating our chain like building friendships within a group like this one?**
■ **What's one thing we can do this week to "strengthen the chain" of friendships within this group?**

Communication

preparation: You'll need access to two or more computers that are connected to the same on-line service with a "chat" function (such as America Online or CompuServe). Determine ahead of time what "room" or area kids will meet in to chat. Form as many groups as you have computers, and have groups meet where the computers are.

description: Have kids who use on-line services regularly sign onto the service and go to the prearranged meeting "room." For example, on America Online, kids might create a private room named "Youth Room" (see various on-line service instructions for help). Then have kids at each computer take turns communicating with the other groups, sharing their answers to the following questions:

- **Who are you?**
- **What do you think about this method of communication?**
- **What's good about this kind of communication? what's bad?**

Tip: *If kids aren't familiar with computers or don't type well, allow them to dictate their answers to someone who's familiar with the computer.* ■

After allowing everyone to communicate, have kids disconnect from the on-line service and meet together in one big group. Have kids form groups of no more than five and tell what they liked and disliked about on-line communication. Then have kids talk together to clarify information they might not have understood when it was discussed on the computer. Ask kids to discuss why face-to-face communication will never be completely replaced by on-line communication.

Then have kids enjoy the best kind of communication of all, a group hug that expresses love for one another.

Tip: *Encourage kids who use on-line services regularly to exchange e-mail addresses so they can communicate with each other during the week. If possible set up a church e-mail address where kids can send messages of encouragement, notes of concern, and prayer requests that can then be given to the appropriate people.* ■

Compliment Contest

preparation: Post a sign saying "Put-Down Free Zone" (or something to that effect) in your meeting room. You'll need newsprint, markers, a sheet listing kids' names, and a small prize for every person.

description: As teenagers arrive give a genuine compliment to each one, and explain that you'll reward them for compliments they give to others during this meeting.

Form four teams, and give each team a sheet of newsprint and a marker. Have teams compete by listing as many ways to build others up as they can think of. After two minutes call time. Encourage kids to use the ideas they've written during the rest of the meeting. Use the following questions to process the activity:

■ **Why is it easier to cut people down than to compliment them?**

■ **Your team benefited from each person's ideas—how does sincere affirmation build up the whole group?**

■ **How can we encourage each other to encourage?**

Challenge kids to find more ways to build each other up, using Hebrews 10:24-25 as the Bible basis for this goal.

At the end of the meeting, give each person an award for complimentary behavior.

Crazy Crossing

preparation: Prepare a list of descriptive phrases such as the following: "I am wearing socks," "My shoes are untied," "I forgot to brush my teeth today," "I got an A on a test this week," "I am an only child," "I am the youngest in my family," and so on.

description: Form two equal teams. Have teams stand against opposite walls of your meeting room, facing each other.

From your prepared list, call out the various descriptive phrases. Tell kids that when a phrase applies to them, they are to run to the opposite side, changing teams. Keep the action level high by keeping pauses between descriptive phrases brief and occasionally calling out phrases that apply to everyone.

Continue until teams are well mixed and kids have learned several things about one another.

Tip: *This crowdbreaker is especially good for shy teenagers since they don't have to talk to unfamiliar people right away.* ■

Deli Creations

preparation: Hang two large rectangular pillows from the ceiling with sturdy twine or rope. Hang them about three feet apart and parallel to one another about two feet off the floor. They will represent pieces of bread for the crowdbreaker.

description: Have kids form a large circle around the hanging pillows. If you have more than 20 people, form two groups with two pillows each. Have each person say his or her name and favorite sandwich ingredient. If someone else has already named that ingredient, the person has to choose another. After everyone has shared, start naming sandwich combinations, using the ingredients kids have already named. You might come up with combinations such as peanut butter and jelly; turkey, Swiss, and tomato; or bologna and cheese. Have kids who named those ingredients earlier race to the middle of the circle to form that sandwich combination, fitting themselves between the two pieces of "bread." Choose outrageous sandwich combinations, and keep things moving. End the crowdbreaker by calling out a sandwich containing all of the ingredients to see if all of the kids can squeeze between the pieces of bread.

e-Mail Me

preparation: No preparation is needed for this activity.

description: Say: **Many people use e-mail to send messages to others through computer networks. Often they choose names and addresses that tell something about themselves. For example, a Christian writer might use the e-mail name "crosscribe." Each person's mailbox is found at a specific location (designated by the @, or "at," sign). This Christian writer's full name and address might be "crosscribe@god's.word." I'm going to guide you in creating e-mail addresses that reflect your interests.**

Form groups of no more than four. Allow time for all group members to answer each question before you move on to the next one. Ask:

■ **To what name and address would we send e-mail about your favorite hobby?**

■ **To what name and address would we send e-mail about your favorite subject in school?**

■ **To what name and address would we send e-mail to ask about** the best trip you've taken during the past few years?

■ To what name and address would we send e-mail to ask about a dream you have for the future?

After kids have discussed the questions, have each group create an e-mail address for God. Then have groups share their ideas.

eyes to See You

preparation: You'll need boxes of toothpicks, boxes of paper clips, and rolls of tape.

description: Form pairs, and give each pair a box of toothpicks, a box of paper clips, and a roll of tape. Say: **You have five minutes to work with your partner to create a pair of glasses you can wear. Go!**

After five minutes have pairs model their creations for the group. Then have pairs discuss these questions:

■ **What did you learn about your partner during this activity?**

■ **How does working together and learning about each other help us "see" each other more clearly in real life?**

■ **What's one way you can begin to "see more clearly" the people around you at church or school this week?**

Tip: *This activity can be completed by just giving pairs handfuls of toothpicks and paper clips. However, the boxes give kids more items to use in making their glasses.* ■

favorites

preparation: Make enough copies of the "Finding Favorites" handout (p. 28) for each group member to have one. You'll also need pencils.

description: When kids arrive, give each person a handout and a pencil. Say: **You have three minutes to fill in the boxes on your handout according to the instructions.**

Call time after about three minutes. If your kids haven't collected many names, give them more time. Then have kids tally their scores and add them all together to determine the group total. Declare that number your group's favorite number, and have kids all congratulate each other for the part each person had in determining that number.

feeling Wall

preparation: You'll need plain paper napkins, tape, and ballpoint pens.

description: Give each person a napkin. Set out the pens, and have each person draw a picture or symbol that illustrates how he or she feels right now. As kids finish have them initial their napkins and tape them to one of the meeting-room walls. When everyone finishes have kids form groups of three and take each other on a tour of the "feeling wall," explaining their napkins to the other members of their trio. Then have trios discuss these questions:

- **What was difficult about drawing on a napkin?**
- **How is the delicate nature of the napkin similar to our feelings?**
- **What can we do on a regular basis to help protect each other's feelings?**

As an ongoing journal of your group members' lives, you can keep the napkins on the wall and add new ones every week.

finding Favorites

Instructions: Interview others in the room to discover their favorite items in the categories on this sheet. In the box with each category, write down the person's name and his or her favorite item. You'll get 5 points for each category in which you list at least one name and a favorite. You'll get 2 points for each additional name and favorite in the same category.

sports	songs	movies	foods
colors	zoo animals	movie stars	musicians
books	authors	news reporters	school subjects
table games	TV stars	cars	places

flaky Races

preparation: You'll need a box of "flake" cereal (such as corn flakes or Wheaties).

description: Have kids gather around a table. Open a box of flake cereal, and have each person choose a flake from the box that somehow represents him or her. For example, someone might choose a round flake because she thinks she's a "well-rounded" person, while someone else might choose a flake with sharp edges because he likes to live "on the edge."

Once everyone has chosen a flake, have kids turn to partners and explain what their flakes describe about them. Then say: **Look very closely at your flake, because in just a moment you're going to have to find it in a pile of other flakes that look pretty much the same.**

Have kids carefully place their flakes in the center of the table, then cover the table with a thin layer of flakes from the cereal box. Say: **When I say "go," you'll race to find your flake. You can do almost anything you want to prevent the other group members from finding their flakes first. But if you break any flake, you're automatically out of the game. Ready? Go!**

When the race is over, congratulate the winner, and allow the rest of the group members to locate their flakes if they want to. Then ask:

■ **Would you consider yourself to be a "flaky" person? Why or why not?**

■ **Do you think that the things that make people unique also sometimes make them seem flaky to others? Why or why not?**

- How is racing to find your special flake in the pile the same as trying to find and develop your own unique qualities in the real world?
- What's unique about you? about the person on your right?

follow the Leaders

preparation: No preparation is necessary for this activity.

description: Form equal groups of about four, and have group members number off. Have each group find one other group and stand face to face, with Ones facing Ones, Twos facing Twos, and so on. Say: **We're going to play a different kind of Follow the Leader. In a moment I'll pick one group from each pair of groups to be the Leader Group and one group to be the Follower Group. The Leader Group's job is to come up with a creative movement for the Follower Group to duplicate. Your goal is to make your creative movement so unique that the Follower Group won't be able to duplicate it. Your movement can last only five seconds, and it must involve every member of your group.**

Here's the real catch: Leader Group members do not all have to do the same movement. You can each do something different, as long as you all move creatively at the same time. Follower Groups, each of your members must follow exactly his or her counterpart in the Leader Group. That means Ones must mirror Ones, Twos must mirror Twos, and so on. If you do your job right, Follower Groups will look like mirror images of the Leader Groups.

Once kids understand choose a Leader Group for each pair of groups, and start the fun. After a minute or two, have groups switch roles. Continue until all groups have had a chance to lead and a chance to follow.

food Fest

preparation: You'll need a variety of prepared foods. Ask church members to donate vegetables, main dishes, and desserts. Let kids know in advance that this meeting or activity will include a meal.

description: Spread the food out on two or three tables (or more if you have more than 30 kids). Then call out the following instructions one at a time, and have kids group themselves accordingly. After kids move have them tell the people around them why they moved where they did.

Here are the instructions to call out:
- **Move to the food that reminds you of how you feel right now.**
- **Move to the food that reminds you most of home.**
- **Move to the food that reminds you of a meal from your childhood.**
- **Move to the food that looks most like you.**
- **Move to the food that best describes you.**

Then tell kids to move to the food they would most like to eat. Have kids enjoy that food item, as well as all the rest.

graffiti Banner

preparation: You'll need a long sheet of craft paper and different colors of spray paint. Choose an outdoor location where kids can safely use spray paint.

description: After kids arrive, say: **Today's your chance to become graffiti artists. We're going to decorate this banner for our meeting area.**

Have each person interview two or three other people about their interests and hobbies then use the spray paint to write words or draw pictures on the banner to represent those people. For example, someone might paint the word "athlete" on the banner to represent a group member's interest in sports, or someone might create musical notes to represent an interest in music. Be sure each group member is interviewed by at least two other people.

When the banner is complete, display it in your meeting room, and have kids guess which group member each word or illustration represents. Even when they guess wrong, they'll discover each other's interests.

Tip: *You might want to caution kids against getting spray paint on their clothes. It will not wash out unless they use paint thinner on it before it dries.* ■

half-Empty, Half-Full

preparation: You'll need uninflated balloons.

description: Distribute one balloon to each person, and ask kids to inflate their balloons to the extent that they feel understood by their families (or friends, members of their church, schoolmates, or any other group you choose). If they feel very understood, the balloon should be nicely full. If they feel others understand them somewhat, the balloon should be half-full. If they don't feel understood at all, the balloon should remain empty.

Then form groups of three or four, and ask kids to answer these questions:

■ **Why did you fill your balloon the way that you did?**
■ **What would it take for you to feel more understood?**
■ **What can you do to help others understand you better?**

Have volunteers share insights from this activity.

If you're presenting a meeting related to this topic, distribute balloons again at the end of the meeting, and repeat the activity. Have kids form groups again and discuss these questions:

■ **If there's been a change in your balloon, what is it? Why?**

■ **What will you do in the next 48 hours to help "fill your balloon" and be better understood by others?**

Tip: *This crowdbreaker works best when you'll be discussing issues such as communication, self-acceptance, and sensitivity to others.* ■

having a Ball

preparation: You'll need beach balls and permanent markers.

description: Form groups of no more than five, and give each group a beach ball and a marker. Have kids take turns telling where they'd go if they could vacation anywhere in the world. Then have each person write on a beach ball panel their names and where they'd like to go. When groups have finished their beach balls, have them pass them around the room to other groups until you say "stop."

If any group has its own beach ball at that point, have kids in that group stand, introduce each other, and tell what they wrote on the ball. If each group has someone else's beach ball, give kids another assignment, such as deciding what they'd buy if they had a million dollars, and have them write their names and that item on the beach ball they're holding. Continue until the balls are covered with information or until all groups have shared.

hoops Course

preparation: You'll need paper, markers, and Hula Hoops.

description: Give each person a sheet of paper and a few markers, and tell kids to decorate their papers with symbols of their hobbies and interests. Then have kids create paper airplanes with their decorated papers.

When the planes are completed, have everyone stand along an imaginary line at one end of a long hall, and throw the planes toward the other end. Place the Hula Hoops on the floor so they encircle as many planes as possible. If some planes can't be encircled with at least one other plane, have the kids who created these planes throw them again, attempting to land them in or near one of the hula hoops. Then have kids whose planes are together in each Hula Hoop form groups and take turns sharing something about the decorations on their plane.

Allow a couple of minutes for discussion, then repeat the activity. If kids end up in a group with someone they were with before, have the kids who were together switch planes and share what they can remember about the symbols on the person's plane.

icebreaker

preparation: You'll need several buckets of ice cubes (crushed ice won't work). Have several paper plates and paper towels handy.

description: Form teams of four or five, and give each team a bucket of ice cubes and a paper plate. Say: **In your team, answer each question I ask you, and write your answer with ice cubes on the paper plate. Raise your hand when your group has each answer spelled out.**

Ask the following questions. After each one, note which team finished first. Ask:

- **Who has the shortest first name?** No nicknames or initials are allowed.
- **Whose birthday is closest to today?**
- **Who has lived in the most places?**
- **Who has lived in the same house the longest?**
- **Who has the oldest brother or sister?**
- **Who has the most change (coins only) in a pocket or purse?**

After questions have been answered, you might want to make shaved-ice treats with unused ice and flavoring. Provide paper towels to dry cold, wet hands.

Ice-Melt Race

preparation: You'll need "sealable" plastic bags (quart-sized or larger), ice cubes, and a fun winter prize such as a mitten or a knit cap. You may want to have a cassette player and Christmas cassettes to provide background music.

description: Form groups of three, and give each trio the same number of ice cubes in a sealed plastic bag. Say: **The first group to completely melt its ice without opening the bag wins a prize. Ready? Go!**

While groups try to melt the ice, play "cold weather" songs such as "Frosty the Snowman" or "White Christmas." Encourage groups to use their body heat to melt the ice as quickly as possible. Award the winning team the prize you've chosen, then have everyone join in a group hug.

Tip: *Don't fill the bags too full of ice, or the teams will spend a long time getting the ice melted. You might want to do a test run yourself in order to determine how many ice cubes to use for the amount of time available for this activity.* ■

if You Were a Dwarf

preparation: You'll need paper and pencils.

description: Open this activity by having kids list as many of Snow White's seven dwarfs as they can. Allow a couple of minutes for kids to write down their guesses, then give the answers: Doc, Dopey, Grumpy, Sneezy, Happy, Sleepy, and Bashful.

Then say: **Now write down the name you think Snow White would give to you if she met you at 3:00 on a typical Sunday afternoon. Also write down the name you'd get if she met you at midnight on a typical Friday. Write your real name on your paper, too.**

After kids have finished writing, collect the papers, randomly read the newly created dwarf names, and have kids guess which group member each name represents. After the names are guessed or revealed, have kids share the reasons they picked the names they did.

i'm Not Who You Think I Am

preparation: You'll need index cards and pencils.

description: Have kids mingle with each other and learn as much as possible about every other member of the group in the time allotted. Encourage kids to discuss the kinds of things they enjoy doing during their free time, the things they like and dislike about school, the shows they watch on television, and the kind of music they like. Make sure kids learn each other's names as well. Tell kids to be sure to talk with every other group member at least once.

After about 10 minutes, have each person write his or her name on an index card. Then have each person choose the group member who he or she learned the most new information about. Have kids write this name on their cards and circle it.

Collect the cards, and read the circled names one at a time, having teenagers who chose that name stand and tell what they learned about the person.

Instant Campgrounds

preparation: You'll need tape; scissors; string; candles; candleholders; matches; and large, plastic trash bags.

description: Use this creative crowdbreaker the next time you want your study time to have a "camp" feel. Once everyone has arrived, set out all of the supplies. Form pairs, and tell kids to work with their partners to create their own personal campsites—complete with "tents" and "campfires."

Have kids use the trash bags, string, chairs, and tape to create their tents, and the candles, candleholders, and matches to create their campfires. Make sure kids face their tents toward the center of the room so everyone can join in the activity easily.

When pairs are finished, have kids vote on special awards for creativity, such as Best Tent, Largest Tent, or Most Creative Use of Plastic. Then, if possible, switch off the main lights, and lead kids through a study using only the light of their campfires.

Tip: *As always when using candles, encourage kids to be careful to keep anything flammable away from the flame.* ■

It's Everyone's Birthday!

preparation: You'll need cake, ice cream, candles, and birthday-party decorations.

description: When kids arrive tell them that today the group will be celebrating everyone's birthday, just for fun. Open by singing "Happy Birthday" (with everyone's name listed as speedily as possible at the appropriate place in the song) and enjoying cake and ice cream. Be sure everyone gets to blow out at least one candle on the cake.

Then have kids sit in a circle and give imaginary "gifts" to one another. Tell kids that they can give any gift they desire. Have kids use the following statement during this gift-giving time: "(Name), I give you the gift of . . . because . . . "

If there are newcomers in the group, encourage kids to give them gifts that might help them to enjoy the group. For example, someone might give the gift of "humor" because it takes a sense of humor to be a part of the group. Make sure everyone receives one gift before anyone receives a second one.

Tip: *This crowdbreaker works well as an introduction to a meeting about self-esteem or learning to be happy with who you are.* ■

Kamikaze

preparation: You'll need scrap paper, pencils, and a trash can.

description: Give each teenager five to 10 sheets of scrap paper and a pencil. Instruct each person to create a fleet of paper airplanes, all of which bear his or her name.

Set up a trash can 20 feet away from the group, and tell kids they're to send their planes on a kamikaze mission to crash into the smokestack of the battleship (the trash can). Have group members call out their own names as they toss their planes toward the trash can. You can have kids do this all at once if they know each other well. If you have a new group, and the kids are still getting to know one another, have them toss their planes one at a time. Determine the winner by collecting the planes that made it into the can and deciding whose name appears most often. Reward the winner with a shower of paper planes sent toward him or her by the rest of the group.

Key Investigations

preparation: Before this activity place treats in a closet or room that can be locked, then lock the door behind you. Be sure you have a key to open the door. You'll also need masking tape, a marker, a pencil, and a sheet of paper.

description: Once everyone has arrived, have each person give you a key (any kind will do). Don't tell the kids why you want the keys, but assure them that they'll get their keys back before the end of the meeting. Use masking tape and a marker to mark each key, using a symbol or number that corresponds with the person whose key it is. Be sure to mark your key to the locked door in a similar manner. Don't let anyone see the list that tells you which key belongs to which person.

Once you have a key from everyone, take the whole group to the locked door. Say: **There's a wonderful surprise behind this locked door. To get to this surprise, all you have to do is find the right key and unlock the door within two minutes.**

Dump all of the keys in a pile on the floor in front of the locked door (don't forget to include the key that opens it). If your group is small, dump several extra keys in the pile to make the task more challenging. On "go," let kids dive in to find the right key. Give no instructions—allow kids to decide on their own plan of action.

If kids find the key within two minutes, allow them to open the door, get the treats, and return to your meeting room for a discussion. If kids fail to find the key before the time is up, stop the action, and have kids discuss the experience right there. Ask:

■ **What was difficult about finding the key to the door?**

■ How is trying to find the right key like trying to find out the truth about God?

■ During the search did you look for your own key and move it out of the way, or did you just choose keys at random to try on the door?

■ How is moving your own key out of the way like guiding someone else toward Christ?

■ What is the "key" to life on earth?

After the discussion, unlock the door, and allow kids to enjoy the treats. And be sure to return the right keys to the right people.

luau's Over

preparation: You'll need Hula Hoops and fresh pineapples or coconuts.

description: Form at least two teams of no more than six, and give each team a Hula Hoop. Place a pineapple or coconut in the middle of the room, and have teams stand in a large circle (about a 15-foot radius) around the pineapple or coconut.

Say: **The object of this activity is to toss your Hula Hoop around the pineapple** (or coconut). **The person who is holding the Hula Hoop may toss it only after calling out all of his or her team members' full names in succession. In other words, when I say "go," the first person in line calls out his or her own name, followed by the**

second person's name, and so on. After calling out the last person's name, the first person may toss the Hula Hoop. Five points will be awarded for each hoop that circles the pineapple (or coconut), **and there will be a bonus of 10 points awarded to the team that tosses the first hoop to make it around the pineapple** (or coconut) **each round.**

Explain that you'll say "go" to start each round and that kids must take turns being the tossers. Play until each group member has had a chance to toss the hula hoop. If you'd like to make things a little crazier, don't keep track of points, and have kids randomly switch teams after each round.

Enjoy the pineapple (or coconut) along with regular snacks after this activity.

mall-Map Madness

preparation: You'll need copies of a map of a local shopping mall. Or you may want to make up and copy a simple map of your own that lists the different stores in a nearby shopping area.

description: Give each person a mall map, and say: **Look over the stores shown on this map, and pick the one that best represents you. It doesn't have to be your favorite store, but the name of the store or the products sold in it should give a clue about who you are. For example, you might pick a candy store because little kids really like you, or you could pick the optical store because you like to "look into" things. If you don't find a store that tells something about you, make one up!**

Have each person tell which store he or she chose and why. Have kids list people's names next to their chosen stores on the map.

After all of the kids have reported, have volunteers tell what they discovered about other group members. For fun, have the kids choose a store that they think represents you or other leaders.

marketing

preparation: You'll need paper, pencils, and a few creative prizes (see "Description").

description: Give kids paper and pencils. Say: **Create a description of yourself, including your interests, hobbies, information about your family, and other tidbits. Use as many brand names as possible in your description.**

For example, if you're writing about your interest in sports, you might include a sentence such as "I have *Mounds* of fun when I *Wisk* away in my *Nikes* to play golf." As often as possible, use the brand names as a part of your description, rather than referring to the actual product. For example, in the sentence I gave you, I used "Mounds" (a candy bar) and "Wisk" (a detergent) as part of the description, but I used "Nikes" to refer to the actual product.

You'll be awarded 5 points for each brand name you use in your description and 1 point for each time you use a brand name to refer to the actual product (like my use of Nikes).

Allow kids five or six minutes to write their descriptions, then have kids read their descriptions aloud for the whole group. Have kids help you count the uses of brand names, and tally the points for each person on a sheet of paper. Award the kids who get the most points with a few brand-name items that have positive names, such as Almond Joy, Mr. Goodbar, or Happy Cat.

mega-Mirror Me

preparation: No preparation is needed for this activity.

description: Form equal-sized groups of 10 or fewer, and give each group a number. Tell the groups they're going to take turns trying to "out-pose" each other. Say: **When I say "go," I want members of Group One to work together to create a pose (or human sculpture) that you think the other groups won't be able to duplicate.**

You'll have 30 seconds to create your pose, then the other groups will have 15 seconds to duplicate it. Ready? Go!

Call time after 30 seconds, and have the members of Group One freeze while the other groups attempt to duplicate their pose. Call time again after another 15 seconds, then inspect the groups to determine which ones accomplished the task. Award each successful group 500 points. If no other group successfully duplicated the pose, award 1,000 points to the group that created the pose. Play until one group accumulates 2,500 points.

a Mile in My Moccasins

preparation: You'll need string or shoelaces.

description: Have each person find a partner by choosing the person in the class whose appearance is the most different from his or her own. For example, a pair could be a burly football player and a petite girl. Once pairs are formed, have partners switch shoes. Say: **You must wear your partner's shoes. That means you must try to put them on, even if they're much too large or much too small. If you absolutely cannot wear your partner's shoes without destroying them, find a way to tie the shoes to your feet.** Have string or shoelaces available for kids who can't wear their partners' shoes.

Once partners have switched shoes, lead the group through your meeting or activity. At the end of the meeting or activity, have the kids form groups of four to discuss these questions:

■ **How do your feet feel?**
■ **What does this experience tell you about judging others?**
■ **Why would it be easier to put ourselves in the shoes of someone who is similar to us than those belonging to someone who is different from us?**
■ **How can we keep ourselves from judging others?**

mirror Images

preparation: You'll need a pocket mirror for each person, index cards, and pencils. You'll also need Bibles and paint pens or permanent markers.

description: Give each person a mirror, an index card, and a pencil. Ask kids to look in their mirrors and privately write everything they see in the mirror on the card.

After a few minutes, form pairs. Direct teenagers to hold the mirrors up to their partners' faces and tell their partners what they see. Have teenagers add their partners' comments to their own cards.

Form new pairs, and repeat this activity. Remind kids to be positive and not to criticize their partners. For example, a teenager might hold a mirror to her partner's face and say: "I see blue eyes that sparkle when you laugh; I see beautiful hair; I see eyebrows that I wish I had; I see teeth that never bite into people."

Afterward have kids form foursomes. Give each foursome a Bible, and have them read Proverbs 15:13 together. Then have groups discuss the following questions:

■ **What did your friends notice about you that you hadn't seen before?**

■ **What factors about your appearance do you have control over?** (Smiling; looking into people's eyes.)

■ **When is a mirror your friend? your enemy?**

■ **How do you think God wants you to think about what you see in mirrors?**

■ **What does Proverbs 15:13 have to say about your appearance?**

Give each person a paint pen or a permanent marker, and have him or her write "Proverbs 15:13" across his or her pocket mirror. Encourage kids to cultivate the habit of seeing good in their appearances and enhancing that good, to look in mirrors long enough to remove spinach from their teeth but not long enough to be critical, and to let caring friends become the most reliable mirrors of their beauty.

move It!

preparation: You'll need a chair for each person. Place the chairs in a circle.

description: After the kids are seated in the circle of chairs, explain that you're going to read some statements that may or may not be true of them. As you read each statement, kids for whom that statement is true must move one chair to the right, even if someone is already sitting there (kids will be sitting on each other's laps in this activity).

Read the following statements—and add your own—to get kids moving:

Move to the right one chair if
- **you're wearing white socks.**
- **you have something in your hair.**
- **you still like to watch** *Mr. Rogers' Neighborhood.*
- **one of your siblings drives you crazy.**
- **you drive your siblings crazy.**
- **you're wearing sneakers.**
- **you got an A on a math test this year.**
- **you forgot to study for a quiz or test this year.**
- **you overslept and were late to school or church at least once this year.**
- **you remembered to brush your teeth today.**

Continue until kids have moved around several times and are ready to settle into your regular meeting.

my Cup Overfloweth

preparation: You'll need one small (3- to 5-ounce) paper cup and lots of jelly beans for each person.

description: Give each person a cup that is half-full of jelly beans. Form a large circle, and have each person in the circle state his or her name, favorite candy bar, and one unusual personal fact. For example, someone might say, "My name is Jonathan, I like chocolate with peanuts, and I have a pet iguana."

After all have shared, have kids take turns challenging others to name one of the facts shared about a specific group member. For example, Terry might challenge someone to name Bonnie's favorite candy bar. If the person challenged remembers the information correctly, he or she may collect two jelly beans from the challenger. If not, the challenger may collect five jelly beans from the person who guessed incorrectly.

At the end of the activity, the person with the most jelly beans wins and gets to help the leader distribute more candy to the whole group.

name Switch

preparation: No preparation is needed for this activity.

description: Have kids form two equal-sized teams. Have teams line up facing each other. Ask each person to trade names with the person across from him or her. Tell kids that they're to be these new people until they trade names again. Then on your signal, have kids randomly rearrange themselves in their teams and line up again. Have kids trade their current names using the following format: "First I was (person's real name), then I became (first partner's name), and now I'm (current partner's name)." Repeat this activity until kids have trouble remembering their lists of names. Keep things moving as quickly as possible. At the end of your meeting or activity, have kids try to remember all of the names they had during the game.

Opposites Attract

preparation: You'll need an index card for each person. On each card write one emotion (such as happy, sad, excited, bored, pleased, depressed, angry, and friendly). Try to include an opposite for each emotion, as kids will be trying to find an emotion that contrasts their own.

description: Distribute one card to each person. Explain that kids must act according to the emotion listed on their cards as they search for someone with the opposite or a contrasting emotion. Tell the kids not to tell what is written on their cards, but to simply pair up with the person they think has the opposite emotion. When kids think they've found their opposites, call time, and have teenagers tell their partners which emotion was on their cards. Ask pairs to talk briefly about a time that they felt the emotion listed on either partner's card.

Shuffle the cards, and repeat the activity.

Photo Fun

preparation: You'll need at least one camera (instant-print cameras or video cameras work best, but any camera will do) and a prize.

description: Ask kids to mill around the room and talk with others, trying to find three other people with whom they share a common interest. When four or more teenagers discover something they have in common, have those kids form themselves into a statue illustrating that activity and call out, "Picture, please." When you hear "Picture, please," take a picture of the statue, and try to figure out what it represents.

You may want the assistance of a few adult helpers (with their own cameras) so you don't miss any photo opportunities. Have kids continue with this activity until you've taken a picture of each person at least once. If possible, display the pictures (or view the video) during the meeting. Award a prize to the person who is featured in the most photos.

picture Me

preparation: You'll need a stack of magazines that have lots of advertisements.

description: Have kids skim through the magazines and tear out pictures that meet the following requirements:

Find a picture that
- **illustrates how you feel right now,**
- **illustrates how you think others see you,**
- **illustrates how you see your friends, and**
- **illustrates what it means to be a Christian.**

Then have kids form groups of no more than five by grouping themselves with others who have at least one similar picture. Have kids tell group members what their different pictures represent.

pizza to Go

preparation: You'll need a small notepad (or small sheets of paper) and a pencil for each person. You'll also need newsprint or a blackboard. This crowdbreaker involves ordering pizza for your group. Plan your activity so that the arrival of the pizzas will coincide with a snack time.

description: After kids arrive give each person a notepad and a pencil. Say: **For the next few minutes, you're going to be a pizza-**

delivery person. Your task is to visit three other people, find out their names and their favorite pizza toppings, and write their orders on your notepads. Then we'll order real pizzas topped with the group's first five topping choices.

After kids have taken each other's orders, have them read the orders aloud, and tally toppings on newsprint or a blackboard. Order the pizzas to enjoy later.

Tip: *To add fun and create goodwill, ask the delivery person's name when the pizzas are delivered. After kids have finished eating, have them write on the pizza box thank you notes to the delivery person and the pizza cooks. Take kids to the pizza shop to deliver their thank yous personally.* ■

precious Moments

preparation: You'll need a camera with a flash. An instant-print camera would be best. Make sure the room is dark enough that the camera's flash will go off when you take a picture.

description: Have kids form pairs or trios. Give kids a topic to discuss with their partners (see the following list). Explain that you'll be going around the room, randomly taking photos of kids who are talking about the topic. Tell kids to freeze in place and stop talking the second they see the flash of your camera. Then have the group whose photo you just took tell the whole group what they were discussing or what they learned about each other.

After these kids tell the rest of the group about their discussion, give teenagers a new topic, have them form new pairs or trios, and repeat the process. Continue until kids have discussed all of the topics (add others if you have time). If you used an instant-print camera, display the photos at the end of the activity.

Topics:
■ what I love about my room at home
■ what makes me really angry

- why I would or wouldn't want to be the President of the United States
- three things I learned in school or youth group during the last year
- why I like or don't like these kinds of activities
- what makes me different from most people in this room

Tip: *If kids don't or can't see the flash go off, call out "freeze" when you take a picture so kids know when to freeze.* ■

product Shuffle

preparation: No preparation is necessary.

description: Explain that you're going to call out a product category and kids will need to form groups according to which brand of that product they use most regularly. For example, if you were to call out "deodorant," kids would have to find out who else uses the brand they use and form a group. ("I Don't Know" or "None" are valid categories.) Have kids discuss in their groups any subject you choose.

Product categories:
- candy bars
- sneakers
- toothpaste
- headache medicine
- shampoo
- soft drink
- fast-food restaurant
- cassette or CD player

Tip: *In the group discussions, you may want to have kids examine a topic related to an upcoming meeting or just discuss topics that would help kids get to know each other.* ■

really Bad Music Introductions

preparation: You'll need old musical instruments—the more obscure they are, the better. Include at least one accordion if possible. You'll probably want to avoid using highly valuable or delicate instruments.

description: Form groups of no more than five, and randomly distribute the instruments to the group members. If you don't have enough instruments for each person to have one, kids can also create their own "instruments" by drumming on chairs or tables or by humming along with the other instruments.

Say: **Each group must create a short song that briefly introduces each of its members to the whole group. In the song you must tell each person's name and one thing about that person that this group probably doesn't know. Lyrics don't have to rhyme, and musical prowess isn't required for this activity.**

Allow 10 minutes for groups to create their songs. Then have them perform the songs for the whole group. Encourage kids to really get into the music. Make sure kids know they can rap (or speak) the lyrics if they choose.

Tip: *If you're short on instruments, have groups share the instruments when it's time to perform. Since kids likely won't know how to play all of the instruments, practicing really isn't necessary. Actually it can be more fun if you don't let kids play the instruments until it's time for them to perform.* ■

Red Light, Green Light

Preparation: You'll need red, green, and yellow paper circles.

Description: As kids arrive explain that green indicates clear sailing, yellow represents concern, and red represents serious doubts. Ask kids to select a red, green, or yellow paper circle—whichever best describes their feelings about their future.

When everyone has chosen a color, form "stoplight" groups—groups of no more than three in which as many of the three colors are represented as possible. Have kids discuss the following questions:

■ **Why did you choose this color?**

■ **What would have to change in your life in order for you to switch to green? red?**

■ **What color do you think Jesus would have chosen if he had walked into our meeting? Why?**

■ **How does your faith influence your choice of colors?**

Screen-head

Preparation: You'll need a video camera, a VCR, and a television. In advance record yourself in your meeting room welcoming kids to a meeting just as you might welcome them "live," only a bit sillier; act as if your head is inside the TV. At the beginning of the tape, record a few seconds of nothing but the background, and then pop into the picture quickly. Make sure the video shows a close-up of your face and the background for your video matches the background which will be behind the television during the meeting. This is especially effective with a large-screen TV. After your video is ready, practice turning on the VCR and the TV and jumping behind the TV so you can time your "screen-head" performance to match the video.

description: When kids have arrived, turn on the TV and the VCR, jump behind the TV, and pretend you're pressing your head into it. Stay hidden behind the TV until your on-screen "double" finishes the introduction and moves away from the screen.

After your silly introduction, have kids use the video camera to record a group screen-head video in which they introduce themselves and each tells about one interest. Save this tape to use as an introduction to the group for newcomers. Add to it as needed.

Shed a Little Light

preparation: Make enough light-bulb shapes out of three or four colors of construction paper for each person to have one.

description: Give each person a paper light bulb. Say: **When we tell others about certain times in our lives, we shed a little light on who we are.**

Have kids form groups of three or four with others who have the same-color light bulb as they do. Say: **Introduce yourself, and tell the others in your group about something that happened to you five or more years ago.**

After kids have shared, have them form new groups of three or four with others whose light bulbs are different colors from theirs. Say: **Introduce yourself, and tell the others something that describes who you are today.**

After the second sharing time, have kids again form new groups of three or four, with exactly two colors represented in each group. Say: **Introduce yourself, and tell the others what you think you'll be doing in 10 years.**

If you have time, have kids trade colors with each other then repeat the whole activity. Afterward have volunteers share something they learned about other group members.

Shut Those Traps

preparation: You'll need a supply of new mousetraps, a pingpong table, and pingpong equipment. If you have more than 25 kids, you'll want to provide a separate pingpong table for each group of 12 to 20 kids.

description: Have kids encircle the pingpong table. Explain that kids will take turns hitting the pingpong ball then moving clockwise around the table. Have two or three paddles at each end of the table if possible. Instruct kids to hand the paddle to the next person after they hit the ball. Before starting set and place three or four mousetraps on each side of the table.

Say: **The object of this game is to keep the ball going back and forth across the table, not to score points. The ball can bounce more than once on each side, but if you hit the ball off the table or miss the ball, you must tell us something about yourself before we continue. Also, if you hit the ball and it sets off a mousetrap, you may choose someone else to share a fact about himself or herself.**

Play until each person has shared at least once. Encourage kids to aim for the mousetraps so they can invite people who haven't yet shared to tell something about themselves.

Tip: *You can tailor this crowdbreaker to a particular topic by giving kids something specific to share when the ball is missed or* *hits a trap. For example, you could have kids tell about a favorite school subject, a memorable vacation, or what they look for in a friend.* ■

Similarity Search

preparation: You'll need music (a cassette player and cassette work fine).

description: Form one large circle, and have kids rotate counterclockwise as the music plays. Periodically stop the music. Each time you do, announce a characteristic such as "people whose birthdays are in the same month as yours" or "people whose favorite types of movies are the same as yours." Then have teenagers interact with others and form groups of kids who all share the same characteristics. A group can be as few as two people. Have groups sit down in a circle, introduce themselves, and talk briefly about their shared characteristics. After about two minutes, start the music again, and have kids rejoin the big circle for another round.

Here are a few characteristics to call out:

- **same shirt color**
- **same shoe size**
- **same first initial**
- **same school**
- **same hobby or interest**
- **same gender**
- **same height** (within 2 inches)
- **same favorite food**

Split-Second Skits

preparation: No preparation is necessary for this activity.

description: Form at least two groups of no fewer than four. Explain that each group will have five minutes to create a short skit according to the following guidelines:

- The skit must repeat each group member's name at least twice.

■ The skit must include some activity or action that represents an interest of each group member.

■ The skit can be no more than three minutes long.

■ The setting must be a location all group members would enjoy.

■ All group members must participate in the skit.

Have groups perform their skits for the whole group.

Tip: *Award a fun prize to each group to recognize kids' creativity and to thank them for their willingness to participate.* ■

Stop 'n' Speak

preparation: You'll need music (a cassette player and cassette work fine).

description: Form two equal groups, and have the first group stand in a circle, facing out. Instruct the second group to form a larger circle around the first group, facing in. Explain that each person in the outer circle must be facing one person in the inner circle.

Play music and have the circles move—the outside circle moves clockwise, and the inside circle moves counterclockwise. When the music stops, have kids pair up with the person standing opposite them and talk with their partner about the topic you give them from this list:

■ **full name**

■ **number of siblings**

■ **birth order**

■ **best friend**

■ **an embarrassing moment**

■ **best vacation**

■ **why you're here tonight**

■ **a prayer request**

Continue in this manner, having kids move and talk with new partners about each new topic.

After kids have discussed the last topic, have everyone sit in one large circle. Ask kids to share something they learned about another person with the whole group.

Stuff War

preparation: You'll need lots of nonbreakable items in an otherwise empty large room such as a fellowship hall or a gym. Your room may include furniture, sports equipment, books, items of clothing, pieces of paper, shoes, and any other items that aren't easily broken. Use masking tape to mark a line down the middle of the room.

description: Form two teams, and place each on either side of the masking tape. Make sure that each side has a similar amount of "stuff." On your signal kids are to try to collect as much stuff as possible from the other team's side of the room. The only rules are that kids can't throw items and they can't take any item from someone who is currently holding it with at least one hand. Have kids play for a specific amount of time, then have them determine which team has the most stuff, and declare that team the winner. Have both teams return the items to their original locations.

Tip: *This crowdbreaker makes a great lead-in to a meeting about materialism or one discussing what it means to be successful.* ■

Superheroes

preparation: You'll need paper and markers.

description: Form trios, and have kids in each trio tell each other what kind of superheroes they would be if they could have one superpower they wished for (such as superstrength, X-ray vision, stretchable limbs, and the ability to fly). Then have teenagers tell how they'd use these superpowers in everyday life.

After trios have shared, ask volunteers to tell about their trio members' abilities and how they'd use them. Then have trios go back to work and come up with a superhero name for each member of the trio, based on what they know about the other trio members or based on information they can gather about the other trio members' interests. For example, someone who enjoys reading might become Bookman or Bookwoman. Have kids create affirming superhero logos for each other based on these names and post them on a wall in your meeting room.

taste and See

preparation: You'll need various food items from within these categories: salty, sweet, fruits, vegetables, dairy products, and meats.

description: Give each student a food item as he or she enters. For example, you might give the first person a banana; the second, a cup of yogurt; and the third, a piece of beef jerky. Encourage students to think of a connection between themselves and their foods. For example, Bill might say that both his name and a banana start with the letter B.

When everyone has arrived, instruct teenagers to form groups according to their food categories (sweets, dairy products, meats, and so on). Then have teenagers take turns sharing their connections to their food items with each other. Encourage group members to offer suggestions to those who haven't thought of a connection or to those who joined the meeting late.

Allow up to five minutes for group sharing. Then allow kids to eat (or trade) their food items.

tattoo Me

preparation: You'll need a supply of temporary tattoos, a supply of water-based face paint, and small paintbrushes. You'll also need makeup removal supplies.

description: Form pairs, and have kids tell their partners three significant things about themselves. Then have each teenager choose a temporary tattoo that best represents his or her partner, based on what the partner said. Have each person apply the tattoo to his or her partner's hand, arm, or face. After each person is tattooed, have kids share the reasons they chose the symbols they did for their partners. Then have kids use water-based face paint to paint symbols or words on other group members to further symbolize each person's interests or hobbies.

Kids can remove their tattoos and face paint with makeup removal supplies or wear them home to show their families.

things That Go Bump

preparation: You'll need candles and matches.

description: Have kids form trios as they arrive. Then give each trio a lit candle, and have each trio sit in a circle on the floor. Turn off the lights so that candlelight is all that illuminates the room. Then have kids take turns answering the following questions in their trios:

■ **What was your greatest childhood fear?**
■ **What helped you to overcome your fear (if you've overcome it)?**
■ **What fear would you like to overcome now?**

After discussing all three questions, have each trio member pray for the person on his or her left. Have trios blow out their candles after all trio members have prayed. While the room is still dark, have kids form a large circle for a group hug.

Tip: *This crowdbreaker is a great introduction to a meeting about overcoming fears or one about trusting God.* ■

thrown Around the World

preparation: You'll need a large world map that can be marked on, a large cork board or a piece of plywood, a length of string, a marker, tape, and a dart. Tape the map onto the cork board or plywood, and set it in your room. Make certain that the dart will stick into the board when it is thrown from a reasonable distance.

description: As kids arrive have each person draw a small circle on the map around a vacation spot he or she would like to visit someday. Then have a volunteer toss a dart at the board until the dart sticks in the board. Using a piece of string to measure, see which circle the dart came closest to. Have the dart thrower find the person who drew that circle and interview him or her about that vacation choice while the whole group listens. Cross out each circle after the person who drew it has been interviewed.

Then choose a new volunteer, and repeat the process, ignoring crossed-out circles. Keep going until everyone has thrown the dart.

totally Cellular

preparation: Make photocopies of the "Totally Cellular" handout (p. 61). You'll need a handout and a pencil for each person.

description: Distribute handouts and pencils. Say: **Create a telephone number that, when converted to its alphabet equivalent, represents one of your interests. For example, if you have an interest in cars, you might create the number 687-8264, which can be converted into the word "Mustang." If the word you create has fewer than seven letters, you may use the number zero to indicate there is no corresponding letter for that number. If you want to use multiple words, you may place a zero between words. You may also use an area code if you**

totally Cellular

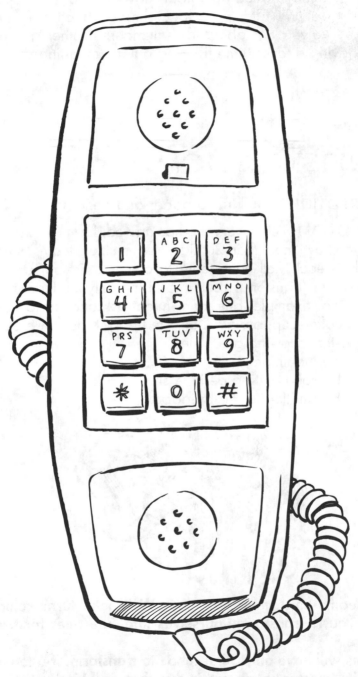

want three more letters to work with. When you've chosen your word or words, write the number on the back of your handout.

After everyone's created a number, have kids form groups of no more than five and attempt to decipher each other's numbers. Allow kids to give clues about their numbers if other group members are having a tough time figuring out the meanings.

transformers

preparation: You'll need paper and pencils.

description: After everyone has arrived, form two transformer teams. If you have more than 20 kids, form multiple teams of no more than 10 kids each. Tell each team to create a list of 10 items for another team to "transform" itself into, using only the team members themselves. For example, one team might ask another to transform itself into a coffee cup, a watch, or a tea bag. Kids can choose any item that fits the following guidelines:

- it must be inanimate;
- it must be solid, with a definite shape; and
- it must be smaller than a breadbox.

Once teams finish their lists, say: **We'll take turns calling out items for you to transform yourselves into. The rules for transformation are**

1. Teams will have only 30 seconds to transform. If a team can't complete its transformation within that time or if I judge their transformation to be substandard, the other team will receive a point. If

the team completes its transformation successfully within 30 seconds, it will receive 3 points.

2. All team members must be a part of the team's transformations. If even one member is left out of a transformation, the other team will receive 1 point.

Once teams understand the rules, start the contest. Continue until the time is up or until teams have attempted all of the transformations. Then tally the scores, and announce a winner.

treasures in the Dark

preparation: You'll need a Bible, a wallet or a purse, a candy bar, a key, and a football or a basketball. You'll also need flashlights (you might want to have kids bring them).

description: Before kids arrive cover your meeting-room windows, and turn off the lights to make the room dark. Then hide all of the items (except the flashlights) around the room.

As kids arrive keep them outside the meeting room. Once everyone arrives give each person a flashlight, and say: **There's something very valuable hidden in this room. Use your flashlight to search the room until you find what you think it is. Once you do, take the item and be seated.**

Send kids into the room, making sure no one turns on the lights. Once all of the items have been chosen or kids have given up looking, turn on the lights. Have those kids who didn't find anything sit near the item they think is the most valuable. Read aloud Matthew 6:19-21, then have kids discuss these questions within their groups:

■ **Why do you think this item is the most valuable?**

■ **What's your reaction to the idea that not everyone agrees with you?**

■ **How does Matthew 6:19-21 relate to this situation?**

■ **What do you treasure most in life? Explain.**

Tip: *This crowdbreaker would work well to start a meeting about setting priorities.* ■

Video Paparazzi

preparation: You'll need a video camera, a VCR, and a TV.

description: As kids are arriving, use the video camera to interview them. Have each person tell his or her name and answer one of the following questions:

■ **What do you wish everybody knew about you that most people don't know?**

■ **What kind of entertainment do you enjoy most? Why?**

■ **Where would you live if you could live anywhere in the world? Why?**

■ **What's the most fun thing you've ever done, and what made it so fun?**

■ **What can other people do to really make your day great?**

As soon as everyone has arrived, play the unedited video. Afterward ask kids how they felt when they were being interviewed. Ask them to compare that feeling to the way they felt when they first came to your group. Then use kids' feelings as a springboard into a discussion of fears, hopes, nervousness, or any other similar topic.

"Watts" up With You?

preparation: You'll need self-adhesive mailing labels and markers.

description: As kids enter have each quickly draw a light bulb on a label. When they've finished drawing, ask them to fill in the wattage, depending on what sort of week they've had. Was it a 40-, 60-, 75-, 100-, or 150-watt kind of week?

Then have kids attach their labels to their foreheads and pair up with someone who chose a different wattage. Have partners discuss reasons they chose the wattages they did. After a minute or two, have pairs pair up to form groups of four, and have each person introduce his or her original partner and explain his or her partner's wattage.

Tip: *This activity is a great lead-in to a lesson about self-esteem or stress.* ■

What a Horrible Day!

preparation: No preparation is needed for this activity.

description: Have kids participate in telling a short story about a character (let kids choose the name) who has just had the worst day in his or her life. Form a circle, and begin the story by saying: **Once upon a time, someone named** (name kids chose) **had the worst possible day anyone could have. It all began when . . .**

Have kids take turns adding terrible things to the character's story—such as breaking a leg, losing a job, and being dumped by a friend—until you've gone around the circle once or twice. Encourage kids to think of things that have gone wrong in their own lives then embellish those situations to make them more crazy and fun. When you're ready to wrap up the story, have the last person end the character's day in a creative way.

Tip: *This crowdbreaker is a great lead-in to a meeting about dealing with difficult times.* ■

What's in That Drink?

preparation: You'll need a large variety of drinks such as punch, soft drinks, milk, water, and juices. You'll also need clear plastic cups, paper, and pencils.

description: Show kids the types of drinks that you have, and ask them to think about which drink is their favorite. Then form groups of about six, and give each group a number. Have kids write their group numbers at the top of their paper. Then have each person write down his or her favorite drink from among the drinks you have displayed without letting other group members see what they've written. Collect the papers, and keep them in stacks by group. Behind a closed door or a curtain, pour equal amounts of each drink listed on the first group's papers into one clear plastic cup. After thoroughly mixing the concoction, show it to the kids, and pour a small amount into a cup for each person in the group.

Have members of that group taste the concoction and write down on new sheets of paper what they think the concoction consists of. For example, in a group of five, kids would each try to guess the mixture's five components. One person might guess that three are Pepsi, one is grape juice, and one is milk.

After kids have shared their guesses, tell the whole group what was really in the mixture. Award 1 point to each person for each item he or she guessed correctly, and total the group's score. Then repeat the activity with the other groups. Give the members of the winning group their choice of the remaining drinks.

Tip: *This crowdbreaker is a great lead-in to a meeting about exploring the uniqueness of each person.* ■

Where Is This?

preparation: You'll need a video camera, a VCR, a television, newsprint, and a marker. Before the crowdbreaker, walk around the church or meeting place, and videotape extreme close-ups of specific items or locations that might be difficult—but not impossible—for kids to find or identify. Before each item or location, videotape a shot of a sheet of newsprint with the words "Where is this?" written on it. Film short clips of about 10 items or locations. Make sure you make a master list of the locations and items so you can verify them when teams figure them out.

description: When kids arrive have them form teams of no more than four. Explain that you'll show kids a short video clip and that they're to guess the location of the clip or the item in the clip. Show only one clip at a time. If no one guesses immediately, let teams search for the item and return when they think they've found it. Award 5 points to the first team to uncover a location. Tally team totals after kids have found all of the videotaped locations or items.

Tip: *This crowdbreaker works well for a meeting held at the beginning of a new year or when the group moves to a new location. It also makes a great introduction to an activity about exploring the hidden talents in your group.* ■

Where Were You?

preparation: No preparation is necessary for this activity.

description: Have kids think about what they were doing at certain times during the day yesterday. Then form groups of no more than four, and tell kids to share with their group what they were doing and where they were at the time you call out. Call out a variety of times, beginning with 5:00 a.m. and ending with midnight.

After calling out two or three times, say: **Change time zones,** and have kids form new groups. Have kids change groups two or three times during the activity.

Write on My Head

preparation: You'll need a large paper grocery bag and a marker for each person.

description: Give each person a paper bag and a marker. Have kids tear eyeholes in their paper bags then place the bags on their heads. Say: **Your job is to discover something about each other group member and write that discovery on that person's paper bag. Or you may draw a picture to illustrate what you discover. For example, if someone tells you that he's interested in cars, you might draw a car on his bag.**

Have kids interview as many people as possible and write or draw something on each person's bag. Allow at least five minutes. Then have kids walk around and read each other's bags before removing and reading their own.

Youth Group Reunion

preparation: You'll need banners, balloons, and decorations for a 25th "reunion" party. Include typical party snacks.

description: Have kids imagine they're 25 years older as they enter the room. Provide punch and other snacks, and encourage kids to find out all they can about each person in the group. Remind kids to act as if they're really older for the duration of this activity. They'll need to make up what happened during the 25 intervening years, based on what they want to see happen.

If kids don't know what to ask each other, suggest that they find out where people are living, what jobs they have, what family members they have, and how things have been going in general.

After the time is up, have kids zoom back to the present and form groups of three. Ask kids to discuss the following questions in their trios:

■ **What did you learn about other group members from this activity?**

■ **How realistic is it to actually reach the goals suggested by this fantasy visit to the future?**

■ **Which one of the people you talked to would you say was the most successful? Explain.**

identity-builders

abstract Group-Photo

preparation: You'll need instant-print cameras.

description: As kids arrive form groups of no more than six. Give each group an instant-print camera. Direct each group to take photos that in some way illustrate your whole group. Explain that the photos can't show any words or any recognizable group members. Allow groups to take up to four photos each to tell their "stories." Encourage kids to be creative and to make the photos as abstract as they want.

Allow groups about 10 minutes to take their photos. Then have groups share their photos with the whole group and explain how the photos illustrate the whole group.

adoration

preparation: No preparation is necessary for this activity.

description: This activity can be pretty intense, so it requires a serious setting and kids who are familiar with each other. Use it with small groups who have gotten to know each other well; otherwise, it may come off as superficial.

Form circles of no more than 15. If you have more than one circle, have groups meet in separate rooms. Sing the song "Father, I Adore You" together, then ask each person to share one reason he or she adores God and one reason he or she adores (or loves) the person to his or her right. Encourage kids to be serious and specific with their affirmations. After everyone has shared, ask:

■ **If we all lay our lives before God, what implications does that**

have for how we relate to one another?

Conclude by praying together as a group, singing the song again as the end of the prayer.

as Fun As . . .

preparation: No preparation is necessary for this activity.

description: Form pairs, and ask kids to come up with creative similes that describe each partner, such as "slippery as a snake" or "friendly as a dog." Then have each pair join another pair and share their similes and reasons for them. Have each new foursome come up with new similes that describe the four people in their group.

End the activity by taking one minute to see how many similes the whole group can come up with that describe the entire group.

bloom

preparation: You'll need two flowering bedding plants for each group member. Have kids bring the plants, or purchase them yourself ahead of time. Be sure to get permission to plant the flowers in an appropriate spot on your church property, and prepare that spot for planting flowers.

description: As kids arrive make sure each has two plants. Then have kids share how they are like or unlike one of the plants they brought or were given. For example, someone might say, "Like this plant, I need lots of attention to grow" or "I'm not like this plant, because my roots are much deeper."

After each person has shared, have kids each take one plant outside and plant it in the area you've chosen. Have kids form a circle around the garden after it is planted, and ask God for continued growth within your group.

After your meeting have each person take one plant home to plant in a garden or flowerpot as a reminder of the garden at church. Encourage kids to remember the flowering and growing youth group each time they water or look at their individual plants.

As often as necessary, have kids take a few minutes to water, weed, and care for the flowers they've planted at church.

Tip: *Use this idea to remind kids of their group identity just before they go their separate ways at the end of a school year or when some members of the group graduate.* ■

Can We Really Do This?

preparation: You'll need Lego sets or any three-dimensional puzzles that require some dexterity to complete. Make sure you have enough for each pair of kids to have one. You'll also need yarn or soft rope.

description: Form pairs, and have partners stand side by side. Help partners tie their inside arms together at the wrist. Then give each pair a Lego set or a puzzle, and explain that pairs are to complete the projects without using their tied-up hands. Walk around, and monitor the activity to be sure kids don't cheat.

Allow plenty of time for kids to work; then call time, and have pairs form a circle by grasping other pairs' free hands with their own free hands. While kids are in this circle, ask:

■ **What was it like to work on a project this way?**

■ **How was this activity like the way we have to work together in the group?**

■ **What are ways that we're "tied together" in this group?**

Care

preparation: You'll need items that could be gifts at a baby shower. Ask kids in advance to bring these items (new or used) to the meeting, or purchase them yourself. Serve refreshments one might enjoy at a baby shower, and decorate the room in baby colors.

description: Have each person show the baby item he or she brought (or choose one from among the ones you purchased or extras others brought) and tell how that item can remind us of the significance of Jesus' birth. For example, someone might choose a safety pin and say, "Because of Jesus' birth, we can feel safe in the world." Or someone might choose a baby sleeper and say, "Jesus' birth signaled an end to sleepless nights when people wondered if they were following God's law the best they could."

After kids have shared, ask:

■ **How might our group have reacted to Jesus' birth had we been living at that time?**

■ **What significance does Jesus' birth hold for this group?**

■ **How can we help each other grow from "newborn" Christians into mature Christians?**

Unless the baby items have to be returned, have kids take them to an agency that can distribute them to needy families.

Tip: *This identity-builder works very well as a tie-in to Christmas.* ■

Cargo Net

preparation: You'll need a cargo net (or a toy net) and string or wire. Attach the net to a section of the ceiling or a wall in your meeting room where it can remain for a long time. Tell kids ahead of time to bring an item that is representative of who they are and that they don't mind giving up.

description: This is an ongoing identity-builder that can help kids to see the history of their group while they affirm the experiences they have together.

Have kids show the items they brought and tell what their items mean to them. Have kids attach their items to the cargo net. Then have kids spend a few minutes in prayer, thanking God for the unique people he's brought together in this group.

Each time you have a meeting or event, have kids add an item to the cargo net that reflects some aspect of that event. For example, if kids go to a baseball game, have them attach a souvenir or ticket stubs to the net.

Over the course of a year, the net will likely become filled with mementos of events and representations of the group's growth and closeness. Have a "net retirement" party at the end of the year, and have kids reflect on each item in the net and choose one or more to take home as a reminder of what the group has meant to them during the year. Repeat the activity each year for lasting impact.

Cassette Intro

preparation: You'll need rulers, markers, 4-inch squares of poster board, a blank cassette tape, and a cassette recorder.

description: As kids arrive give each a poster-board square. Provide several rulers. Direct kids to fold the poster board like a cassette-tape insert card (see example below).

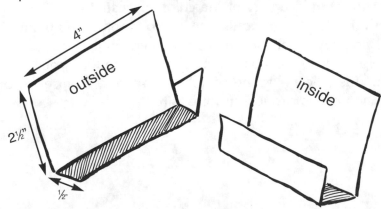

outside — 4" — 2½" — ½"

inside

Ask kids to design covers for a cassette introducing your group to prospective group members. Encourage kids to illustrate aspects of the group on the cover and list on the back of the card real or imaginary song titles that refer to the group's unique qualities. Have kids list any other information that would help an outsider know more about the group.

Then have kids tell about their cassette covers and choose elements they'd like to have on a real cassette describing the group (such as the group's name, meeting times, and favorite group activities). If time permits, have kids record these elements onto a tape. Create and photocopy a cover that includes these elements, and make copies of the tape for kids to give away to friends.

Chip Creation

Preparation: You'll need a variety of snack chips and dips.

description: Have kids sit around a table with a clean surface. Pour a bunch of chips onto the table within reach of the kids. Place a few containers of chip dip on the table, too. Then say: **You have seven minutes to create a sculpture out of chips and dip that illustrates the greatest strength of this group. Go.**

Don't give any further instructions. After the time is up, have kids explain what they created and what it represents. Ask:
- **What was easy about this activity? What was difficult?**
- **How is creating this sculpture like the way we build our group?**
- **What might the fragility of the chips represent in our group?**
- **What's the "dip" that holds our group together? Explain.**

Ask kids to pray silently for the relationships in the group, asking God to help them support one another and keep the group strong. Then have kids "dig in" to the sculpture and feed themselves on a representation of the group's greatest strength.

Community Spices

preparation: You'll need a large assortment of spices.

description: Set out the spices. Have kids take turns smelling each of the spices and choosing one spice that they think best describes their personalities. Once everyone has chosen a spice, have kids each explain their choice to the group. Read aloud 2 Corinthians 2:14-17, then form pairs to discuss the following questions:

■ **What do you think it means to be the "fragrance of Christ"?**

■ **Can we be different from each other, yet still live like Jesus? Why or why not?**

■ **How does your partner's "fragrance" remind you of Christ?**

Call everyone back together. Place a small portion of each spice in a bowl, mix the spices together, then pass the bowl around for everyone to smell. Say: **Even though we all chose different spices, when they are mixed together, they still smell good. In the same way, the people who make up the Body of Christ are like many different fragrances, but when we all work together, we re-create the aroma of Christ for the world.**

Connected

preparation: Obtain a map of your local area (one that includes the locations of all group members' homes), and mount it on cardboard or foam-core art board. You'll also need colored thread, pushpins, pens, and tiny strips of paper.

description: Have each person write his or her name on a strip of paper and use a pushpin to attach the paper to the location on the map of his or her house. Mark the location of the church with another pin. Then have each person use the thread to connect the church location to his or her own marker on the map.

Ask:

■ **What does this map tell us about one way that we're connected to each other?**

■ **What are some other ways that we're connected?**

■ **How we can use this connectedness to reach out to people in our own communities?**

Post this map in your room as a reminder of kids' connection to each other through the church. Add new pins as kids join the group, and move pins around if kids move. Periodically have kids look at the map and discuss new ways to reach out to people in the area.

Cookie Sheets

preparation: You'll need Bibles, sandwich cookies, and poster board.

description: Form trios, and give each trio a sheet of poster board and several sandwich cookies. Have kids read Ephesians 4:25-32. Then say: **Open the cookies, and stick the side with the icing to the poster board. Position the cookies to show ways that we can stick together as a group and encourage each other to live for Jesus. You may fold, tear, or bend the poster board to make your point. Use any verse from Ephesians 4:25-32 as the theme for your "cookie sheet."**

Have trios display their completed cookie sheets for the rest of the group. Applaud each creation, and reward kids with cookies to eat. Then have kids discuss the following questions in their trios:

■ **What sweet results will we experience when we build a group like the ones you've described?**

■ **When are we tempted to eat at each other or tear each other apart as we did with these cookies?**

■ **How can the things symbolized on your cookie sheet free us to cherish each other instead?**

Cut It Out

preparation: You'll need scissors and paper.

description: Have kids pair up and sit back to back. Give each teenager a sheet of paper and a pair of scissors. Say: **Talk to your partner, and share at least three or four favorite activities or interests.**

Give partners a couple of minutes to talk. Then say: **Without talking anymore or peeking at your partner's work, attempt to cut out a shape that illustrates an activity or interest you both share. You may choose from the following shapes and the interest each shape represents:**

■ **A square represents quiet, solitary activities such as reading or watching television.**

■ **A triangle represents creative endeavors such as writing, drawing, or building things.**

■ **A circle represents athletic activities.**

■ **A half-circle represents talking with friends.**

■ **A diamond represents shopping or dreaming of things to own.**

When you're both finished cutting, turn and face each other to see if your shapes match.

After pairs try this once or twice, form new pairs, and repeat the activity. Encourage kids not to give each other hints about which shape to cut out. When the second pairs are finished, have teenagers collect their shapes and stand in a circle, holding up all of the shapes they cut out. Have kids look around the group to see whose shapes theirs match.

Ask:

■ **How does looking for the ways that we're similar to each other help us to know and enjoy each other?**

■ **How does recognizing our similarities help us to grow together as a group?**

■ **How do the differences in our interests add to our group?**

dial-a-Discussion

preparation: Prepare a calendar with group members' names and phone numbers assigned to specific days. Repeat the names and numbers to fill at least three upcoming months on the calendar.

description: Help each group member to select a few favorite Scripture passages. Then have each person list a different reference on each day his or her name appears on the calendar. Make photocopies of the calendar, and give them to the kids.

Have kids each choose specific days during the coming three months to be their "On-Call Discussion" days. Based on the number of kids in your group, tell kids how many days each must choose in order to fill up all the days on your calendar. Kids must choose a different person for each day they select, and no one may select days on which his or her own name appears. Have kids circle their selected days on their own calendars and initial the same days on the master calendar.

Ask kids to call the person listed on the calendar on their circled days and discuss the meaning of the Scripture passage listed. Periodically ask kids how they're doing with their phone calls.

Tip: *Calling kids they don't know very well may be tough for some group members. Don't be too hard on them if they skip a call; just encourage them to try it.* ■

draw on Me

preparation: You'll need white T-shirts and a bunch of fabric paints. Make sure you use fabric paints, as many other markers will bleed through the T-shirts.

description: Have kids put on the T-shirts. Then say: **Think about what you truly value in this group. It can be something a particular person does or something that the group as a whole provides for you. Then silently decorate each other's T-shirts according to the following guidelines:**

■ **If you appreciate something an individual does, write a short note on one of his or her T-shirt sleeves describing what you appreciate.**

■ **If you appreciate something that the group as a whole provides for you, write what you appreciate on at least three T-shirt backs.**

■ **If you see someone with nothing written on his or her shirt, write something you appreciate about that person on his or her T-shirt sleeve.**

Remind kids to remain silent as they write.

After kids have done plenty of writing, have them read the items written on others' sleeves and backs. Encourage kids to always show appreciation for the good things individuals do to make the group grow. Have kids wear their decorated shirts at special group events.

dreaming

preparation: No preparation is necessary for this activity.

description: Begin by having kids lie down on the floor and pretend they're watching the clouds go by. If weather permits, consider taking the kids outside for this activity. Give the following instructions, allowing time for kids to complete each one:

■ Think about what you would become if you could be anything in the world.

■ Scoot over next to a partner, and tell him or her what you would become and why. Then brainstorm what you and your partner would become together if you could be anything in the world. When you agree on something, move close to another pair and share what you came up with, and brainstorm what the four of you would be together.

Have kids keep joining others until all kids are next to each other and have come up with a dream of what they would all be together.

dream Rooms

preparation: You'll need masking tape and pens.

description: Distribute masking tape and pens, and have kids scatter throughout the room and sit on the floor. Say: **On the floor, use your tape to create a miniature floor plan for your "dream" bedroom. Include the shape of the room and all of the furniture you want in it, and label everything by writing on the masking tape.**

When kids are finished, have the group tour all of the rooms. Then discuss these questions:

■ What's the best thing you saw on this tour?

■ What do these dream rooms tell you about the people in this group?

■ How is designing your dream room like designing a plan for your whole life?

■ A dream room can be a safe haven for us when the world gets stressful or painful. How can our meeting room become a safe haven for all of us?

encore

preparation: No preparation is needed for this activity.

description: Form two teams. If you have more than 30 kids, you may want to form multiple teams with about 10 kids on each team.

Have teams sit about 20 feet apart while you stand in the middle. Say: **We're going to play a game that requires you to be incredibly creative and to work together as a team. I'm going to give one team a word or a category. That team has to think of a song that either uses that word or applies to the category.**

As soon as the first team thinks of a song, its members will stand up and sing a few lines from it, including the line that applies to the word or category. When the first team finishes, the other team has 15 seconds to come up with another song that meets the same requirement. We'll continue from team to team until a team can't think of a new song within 15 seconds. At that time, the last team to have come up with a song gets 1 point.

Begin the activity by giving one team the first word. Consider using the following words or categories:

- love
- baby
- joy
- toddler songs
- fast-food jingles
- country and western songs
- heart
- beautiful
- Jesus
- help me
- I did it
- only you

eye to Eye

preparation: No preparation is necessary for this activity.

description: Form pairs, and have partners stand facing each other. Have them silently stare into each other's eyes for 60 seconds then discuss these questions:

■ **What's your reaction to this experience?**

■ **Why is it so difficult to look someone in the eye? to be looked at so intently?**

Read aloud Matthew 6:22-23. Then ask:

■ **How is the eye the "lamp of the body"?**

■ **What's one positive quality you see in your partner that's like a "light" shining from his or her life?**

■ **How can this experience help you to love others more? to allow yourself to be loved more by others?**

the Fabric of Faith

preparation: Have each person bring a recent photo of himself or herself to the meeting. Or have a student who is interested in photography take individual pictures and have them developed before the activity. Bring a 3×4-foot piece of burlap or loosely woven fabric in a neutral color. You may need a larger

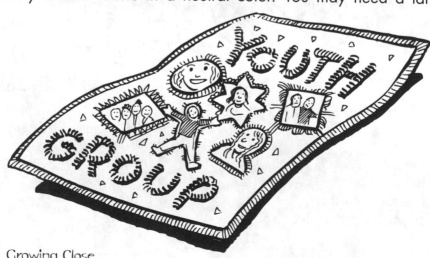

piece of fabric if you have more than 25 kids. You'll also need large needles and 3- to 4-foot lengths of different-colored yarn, string, or wire.

description: Have kids weave yarn into the fabric to "write" the name of the group. Then have each person make a "frame" for his or her photo by weaving string, yarn, or wire into the fabric (see illustration on previous page). Encourage kids to be creative as they make their frames and to allow them to connect with other kids' frames. Hang the picture banner in the room to remind kids of the way that they're woven together in the fabric of faith. Add more pictures as kids join the group.

find It

preparation: No preparation is necessary for this activity.

description: Explain to students that they will be going on a scavenger hunt without leaving the room. They'll be looking for items they can find on their clothes, in their pockets, or on their bodies. Tell kids that the first person to find each item wins that round, but they should all keep the items they collect. See if kids can find the following items:

- several hairs
- a wallet-sized photo of somebody else
- an ID card
- a colorful thread
- a key

After kids have collected these items, form groups of no more than five, and have them discuss the following questions:

- **How are your hairs similar to other group members' hairs? How are they different?**
- **What does the person pictured in your photo mean to you?**
- **Where is the ID from, and what does it say about what you do or where you go?**
- **What does the thread say about what you like to wear?**
- **What does the key open? What does that place mean to you?**

follow Me, Follow You

preparation: No preparation is needed for this activity.

description: Form pairs, and have partners stand face to face. Say: **For the next 60 seconds, you're to remain silent and become a human mirror, doing exactly what your partner does. Ready? Go!**

After 60 seconds, have pairs discuss these questions:
- **Which of you ended up becoming the leader of your pair?**
- **How did the two of you decide who would lead?**
- **How is that similar to the way you operate in real life?**
- **How is that similar to the way you operate within this group?**
- **Are you happy with the role that you play in this group? Why or why not?**
- **What can you do to help your partner to better fulfill the role he or she wants to play within this group?**

To close the activity, read aloud Philippians 2:3-4.

gab Box

preparation: You'll need a box of varied objects, the more unusual, the better. Objects could be anything from a pencil to a car part.

description: Have kids sit in a circle. Set out the box, and read one of the statements below. Have each person choose an item that fits the description and explain why he or she chose that item. Say:

Choose an item that
- **represents who you are.**
- **best symbolizes the strengths of this group.**
- **symbolizes what we could improve in our youth group.**
- **represents your greatest talent.**
- **represents your greatest need.**

Repeat the activity, using another of the statements.

Tip: *Use this activity periodically, placing different items in the Gab Box for kids to choose.* ■

the Golden Rule

preparation: You'll need separate slips of paper with each group member's name written on one. You'll also need note cards and pencils.

description: Give each person a note card and a pencil. Have kids write on their cards one thing they wish someone would do for them or an act of kindness that would encourage them. Explain that these actions must be things that other members of the group could do for them during the meeting. For example, kids might write, "Give me a back rub" or "Pray for me."

Then give each person a slip of paper with someone else's name on it. If someone gets the slip with his or her own name on it, have the person exchange with another person. Say: **We're going to practice the golden rule, which is "Do unto others as you would have them do unto you." Read what you wrote on your card, and then complete that action for the person named on your slip of paper—unless that person would feel uncomfortable being the recipient of that action.**

Allow several minutes for interaction, then ask:

■ **How did it feel to do for someone else what you really wanted someone to do for you?**

■ **What made it difficult or easy to do?**

■ **Why do you think Jesus gave us the golden rule?**

graduation-Cap Toss

preparation: You'll need a graduation cap.

description: Form a circle. Have a volunteer stand in the center of the circle and hold the graduation cap. Have the volunteer spin around and then toss the cap to anyone in the circle. Whoever catches the cap or whoever it falls nearest must say one thing he or she hopes the person in the center of the circle will remember from youth group when he or she "graduates" from the group. This could be an event or activity from the past, something yet to come, or a general lesson learned from being a member of the group. For example, someone might say, "I hope you'll remember the great time we had during the trip to Florida" or "I hope you'll remember how we support each other in this group and that we're still here if you need us."

After someone shares, have that person move to the center of the circle. Repeat the activity until each person has been in the center. It's OK if kids catch the cap more than once; this will force them to think of additional things group members can gain from the group.

group Flag

preparation: You'll need a large piece of material cut into a flag shape, scraps of cloth, needles and thread, scissors, and fabric paint. To make the project look nicer, hem the edges of the cloth so it won't fray.

description: Have kids work together to create a flag that symbolizes things they have in common as well as their own unique qualities. Encourage kids to discuss what they'll place on the flag before they begin working on it. Then make sure everyone is involved in the creation of the flag. Allow kids to add their own contributions to the flag, but be sure that everything that is added to the flag reflects something about the group as a whole or an individual group member.

Display the flag in your youth room as a reminder of the uniqueness of the members of your group as well as the things they have in common.

group Socks

preparation: You'll need several pairs of white athletic socks in sizes that will fit teenagers and fabric paint.

description: Distribute a pair of socks to each group member. Have kids form pairs, and have each share the quality or personality trait that makes him or her valuable to the whole group. Then have each person choose for his or her partner a symbol that illustrates the partner's chosen trait and draw it on one of the partner's socks.

Form a single group, and have the kids choose one symbol that identifies the entire group's common beliefs or interests. Then have each person copy that symbol onto the other sock and put on both socks, wearing the unique symbol on the left foot and the common symbol on the right foot. Let kids mingle and look at each person's unique symbol. Encourage kids to wear the socks periodically as a reminder of the special qualities each brings to the group.

an Honored Guest

preparation: You'll need an instant-print camera and party decorations and supplies.

description: Form groups of no more than six, and have kids brainstorm reasons to honor each person in their group. For example, kids might honor someone for having the most consistent attendance or for driving the longest distance to meetings. Encourage kids to think of a unique and positive honor for each person.

Then have kids use the decorations and supplies to honor the others in their groups with a brief party celebration. Take a photo of each person being honored, and display the photos in the front of the room.

Allow kids to take their photos home as reminders of the honors they received.

hoop Hysteria

preparation: You'll need one Hula Hoop for every 10 people.

description: Have kids choose a leader then stand in a circle and grasp hands. If you have more than 15 kids, form multiple groups of about 10.

Place a Hula Hoop over the head of the group leader. Leave one side of the Hula Hoop resting on the joined hands of the leader and the team member on his or her left. Tell the leader and the person on his or her right to let go of each other's hands so that the other side of the Hula Hoop falls to the ground. Then have them rejoin hands (see the illustration on the previous page).

Explain that the Hula Hoop must be passed over everyone's head and around the circle without anyone letting go of anyone else's hands. To accomplish this, kids must agree on a strategy and cooperate with each other. Time kids to see how fast they can move the hoop around the circle.

Play several rounds, and let kids try to improve their times.

Identity Quiz

preparation: Prepare a list of positive attributes that describe individual kids in your group. Here are a few to consider:

He or she . . .
- makes us laugh.
- goes with the flow.
- has a great smile.
- never complains.
- is a true athlete.

- always listens.
- can be counted on to help out.
- asks great questions.
- likes to spend time with friends.

Make sure you have at least as many attributes as people who will attend; it's OK to repeat attributes. List attributes along the right side of a sheet of paper, and list kids' names alphabetically on the left side of the paper, including a few blank spaces to fill in for visitors. Make photocopies of this handout.

description: Give each group member a pencil and a copy of the handout. Have kids fill in the names of people in attendance who aren't listed on the handout. Explain that kids are to match each person listed on the left side of the paper with an attribute on the right. Tell kids that there are no "right" answers but that they should choose only one person for each attribute.

Allow plenty of time to complete the handout. Then have everyone form a circle. Starting with the last name on the list, have kids tell which attribute they matched to that person and why.

If the Food Fits . . .

preparation: Ask kids to each bring $3.

description: Take kids to a grocery store. In a quiet spot in the parking lot, form pairs. Say: **While you are in the store, choose and purchase a food item that best represents something you appreciate about your partner. You may spend no more than $2.**

Caution kids to be polite in the store, and give them a specific time to meet back in the parking lot. Then have them split up and do their choosing and purchasing individually. When kids have returned to the parking lot, have each person show and explain what he or she purchased.

When everyone has shared, have partners pair up again and return to the store to purchase one food item together that describes how they feel about the youth group as a whole. Let kids know that they may spend no more than $2 together. Have pairs return at a specified time to show what they purchased and tell what it represents.

Then return to your meeting room and enjoy the food or donate it to a food pantry.

I Never Knew That

preparation: You'll need paper and pencils.

description: Give kids paper and pencils. Have kids complete the following sentence on paper with an exaggerated version of something that really happened to them: "The most amazing thing I ever did was . . . " For example, someone who climbed a local hill or mountain might finish the sentence by saying, "The most amazing thing I ever did was to climb Mount Everest with a broken leg."

Collect the papers, and read them aloud. After reading each one, have group members guess whose paper it was and what element of the story is true. After reading all of the papers, have kids each share one thing he or she would like to accomplish in the future. Then close the identity-builder by having teenagers brainstorm activities they'd like to accomplish as a group during the coming year.

Isaiah 6

preparation: You'll need song books with familiar praise or worship songs in them. If possible, have accompaniment for the songs. You'll also need Bibles.

description: Choose someone in your group to be a song leader. Use the songs suggested in the directions, or help the song leader choose appropriate songs to include with the reading. Give each person a reading assignment, and explain how each section is to be read (see directions below). Involve everyone by having groups of kids read sections in unison.

■ Read Isaiah 6:1-3 in a quiet, hushed tone.
■ Sing "Great Is the Lord" or a similar group favorite.
■ Read Isaiah 6:1-5 in an excited voice as a person who feels overwhelmed by the situation would.

- Sing "Humble Thyself in the Sight of the Lord" or a similar group favorite.
- Read Isaiah 6:1-7 in a less excited voice, with an emphasis on the word "I" wherever it appears.
- Sing "Lord, I Lift Your Name on High" or a similar group favorite.
- Read Isaiah 6:1-8 quietly, with an emphasis on the word "Lord."
- Sing "Here I Am, Lord" or a similar group favorite.

After the reading and singing, discuss these questions:
- **How do you think Isaiah felt after this encounter?**
- **Have you ever felt that you were in God's presence? What happened?**
- **How are we as a group like Isaiah in this passage?**
- **Where might God want to send this group? Explain.**

∎t's in the Bag

preparation: You'll need a paper grocery bag, tape, paper, and pencils.

description: Set a grocery bag in the middle of the room. Make sure it stands open so kids can toss papers into it.

Have each person list two prayer requests on separate pieces of paper. Then have kids fold these requests two or three times so they can be easily thrown.

Have kids stand in a circle around the bag, at least six feet away. On your signal, have kids attempt to toss their requests into the bag.

Pick up the bag, and read aloud the requests that made it into the bag. Then have kids pair up to discuss the following questions:
- **How would you feel if only these requests were actually heard by God?**
- **What's a more realistic picture of the way that God listens to our prayer requests?**

Say: **Sometimes the answers to our prayers aren't obvious right away, or they aren't the answers we were hoping for. But God** always hears our prayers and answers them. **Waiting for answers is difficult, but we can help each other by supporting each other in our prayer lives.**

Have each person choose two papers from the bag or the floor then read the requests, and pray silently for the people who made those requests. Then ask kids to think of practical ways to support each other. For example, kids might meet weekly to share prayer concerns and answers to prayer.

Encourage kids to trust that God is listening and responds to every prayer.

It's Like This

preparation: You'll need photocopies of the "It's Like This" handout (p. 98) and pencils.

description: Give each person a pencil and a copy of the "It's Like This" handout. Say: **In order for us to grow as a group, it's important for everyone to understand what each group member believes about God. But it's not always easy to get that kind of discussion going. So we're each going to complete this handout then share it with other group members so we can all discover new things to talk about and grow from. This is not a test to see how much you know or how spiritual you are. A sincere "I don't know" is a valid answer to any of the questions.**

After kids have completed the handout and shared with other group members, post the papers around the room for others to read. Encourage kids to use these handouts as a way to start discussions about their faith.

It's Like This

Complete the following survey. Then find two other people to meet with, and share how you completed each sentence and why you chose the answers you did.

1. God and I
   a. are just getting to know each other.
   b. have been in touch for as long as I can remember.
   c. are, for the most part, strangers.
   d. _____.

2. My favorite characteristic of God is
   a. his love.
   b. his understanding of everything and everybody.
   c. his desire that we do what's right.
   d. _____.

3. I think of God as a _____ because _____.

4. I feel closest to God when
   a. I'm alone.
   b. I'm with other Christians.
   c. I'm out in nature.
   d. _____.

5. One thing I wish I understood better about God is _____.

6. The first thing I'd ask God if I met him face to face would be
_____.

license Plates

preparation: Make cardboard rectangles that are approximately the size and shape of car license plates. You'll need one cardboard rectangle and a set of markers for every four people.

description: Form groups of four, and have each group create a license plate that represents your group as a whole. Encourage kids to create realistic license plates that creatively express the youth group's identity. For example, a group might create a plate that reads "WELV2EAT" (we love to eat).

When everyone is finished, have groups exchange license plates and guess their meanings. Continue until all of the groups have seen all of the license plates.

Return license plates to their original groups, and have kids explain their true meanings. Conclude the activity with a discussion about the group's purpose.

living Altars

preparation: For this identity-builder, you'll need to bring a plant to donate to the meeting room. Choose a hardy variety with large leaves, and make sure the plant has many more leaves than the number of kids you expect to attend the meeting. Set the plant in the center of the room, and circle chairs around it. You'll also need permanent markers and a Bible for each person.

description: Once everyone arrives, have a volunteer read aloud Romans 12:10-18. After the volunteer is finished reading the passage, distribute Bibles, and have kids each read the passage again and choose one way they are going to begin to live out something in that passage.

Then distribute permanent markers, and say: **As a sign of your commitment, write your initials and the appropriate Scripture reference on one of the leaves of this plant. Then, as we watch the plant grow, we can be reminded to let our commitment grow as well.**

After kids write on the leaves, place the plant in a spot in your meeting room that gets natural light. Ask a different teenager to water the plant each week. Allow kids who were absent the first time you did this to add their initials and Scripture references during upcoming weeks. Once or twice a month, have kids gather around the plant and ask God to help their commitments grow.

look at Us Now!

preparation: Prior to the meeting, instruct kids to bring their funniest-looking elementary school pictures. You'll need tape and a sheet of cardboard or poster board on which all of the pictures can be arranged.

description: Allow time for kids to look and laugh at one another's pictures. Then instruct them to arrange all of the pictures on the cardboard or poster board.

After the pictures have been arranged, display them at the front of the meeting room.

Ask:

■ **What can you accomplish as teenagers that you couldn't when you were that age?**

■ **How are you more influential now than you were then?**

■ How are you closer to God? more creative? wiser? more mature?

■ What goals can you set for our group this year that you wouldn't have even thought of then?

Tip: *This activity is great around the beginning of a new year or at the beginning of the school year.* ■

lost and Found

preparation: You'll need paper and pencils.

description: Have kids each write down a personal item that means a lot to them, such as a stereo, a Bible, or a piece of jewelry. Tell kids not to let the rest of the group see what they wrote. Have kids fold their papers as many times as possible. Collect all of the papers, then have everyone leave the room. While kids are gone, hide all of the papers in the room.

Invite the kids to return. Say: **Find a paper that another group member "lost," and try to return it. You may pick up only one paper at a time, and you must try to give it to the person you think lost it. If a paper someone offers you isn't yours, simply say, "Not me." When you receive the right paper, briefly tell the person who gave it to you why the item means so much to you.**

After everyone has his or her own paper back, form a circle and have kids discuss the following questions:

■ **What did you learn about group members in this activity?**

■ **What can we learn about the whole group from this activity?**

■ **How did you work together to return each other's papers? How is that like the way we can work together in everyday circumstances?**

mask Over Me

preparation: You'll need heavy-duty aluminum foil.

description: Form pairs, and give each person a large square of heavy-duty aluminum foil. Say: **With your foil, create a mask of your partner's face by molding the foil to his or her face. Make sure to gently poke holes where your partner's nose and mouth are so he or she can breathe while you work. Ready? Go!**

Once the masks are complete, form a circle, and have kids display their creations. Then say: **Let's go around the circle, and when we come to you, hold up your mask and tell us about the most common mask you wear in real life. For example, you might pretend to be happy even when you're sad. Or you might act as if your family life is good, even though your parents fight all the time.**

After everyone has shared, have kids remove their masks, then each turn to a partner to discuss these questions:

■ **What's one thing this group can do to help you trust more?**

■ **What's one thing you can do to help the group understand you better?**

When pairs finish, have them hang their masks on a wall of the meeting room. Say: **These masks will stay on the wall to remind you to leave your "masks" at the door when you come to a group meeting or event. You don't have to pretend with us because we all love you for who you really are.**

a Measure of Our Group

preparation: You'll need paper, pencils, measuring tapes, rulers, and other measuring devices.

description: Have kids work together to calculate the cumulative group height (total of all group members' heights), the cumulative group hat-size, the cumulative group arm-span, the cumulative group neck-size, and the cumulative group hand-size (measured from the wrist to the tip of the longest finger).

Have kids list these measurements (in inches or centimeters) on a sheet of paper. Then have kids brainstorm the five greatest strengths of their group and choose which measurement corresponds to that strength. For example, kids might say that the greatest measurement represents the group's love for others. Have kids discuss these strengths until they can agree on the ranking of the strengths. If the kids can't agree, allow them to assign more than one strength to each measurement.

Close the activity by thanking God for the measure of good qualities that he has given to your group. Ask for guidance in helping these strengths and others to grow during the coming months.

miracles

preparation: You'll need Bibles.

description: Form groups of no more than five, and have each group read about some of Jesus' miracles. A few passages to consider include John 2:1-11; Luke 5:1-11; Matthew 9:18-26; Matthew 9:27-31; and Mark 8:22-26.

Then ask groups to discuss what kinds of miracles we still see today. Have volunteers share their ideas with the whole group, then ask:

■ **What kinds of miracles does our group need right now?**

■ **What supernatural events has our group already experienced?**

■ **What miracles do you want to happen in the lives of your friends, family members, and others?**

Have kids spend time in prayer, asking God to work the miracles they would like to happen.

mystery Massages

preparation: You'll need blindfolds.

description: Blindfold half of your group members. Then have each of the kids who aren't blindfolded silently move to stand with his or her back toward one of the blindfolded kids. Have each blindfolded person give a shoulder and neck massage to the group member who is standing in front of him or her. Encourage kids to remain silent.

After kids have given a one-minute massage, mix up the group, and then have kids remove their blindfolds. Say: **Based on what you felt as you gave your massage, find the person who you massaged.**

Once kids have all found their partners, have the groups switch roles. After the second round of massages, have kids locate the people they massaged. Then have those pairs discuss these questions:

- How did you identify the person you massaged?
- What do you like about the fact that we're all so different?
- How is the fact that we're all so different like differences in the way we serve others as Christians?
- What's one way your partner serves others in this group?
- What's one way you can serve the people in this group better?

name Maze

preparation: You'll need markers and lots of paper.

description: Give each person several sheets of paper and a marker. Have everyone write out his or her first name, using one sheet of paper for each letter. Then have kids work together to form a large, intersecting maze of names on the floor as in a Scrabble game. For example, Michael may place his letters on the floor horizontally, then Mandy might place hers (except for the M) vertically, starting with the M in Michael.

Let kids know that all names must connect and no names may be placed directly next to one another (either vertically or horizontally) unless all of the letters that connect also form words or other names.

Since this can be quite a challenge for a large group, allow kids to add words that describe group members (such as "kind," "noble," or "friendly") if needed to connect names. When the giant name-connection is complete, have kids discuss the following questions:

- How is the way our names connect like the way we can connect as a group?
- What does the way we worked together on this project say about us?
- What can we learn about our group from this activity?

the Never-Ending Story

preparation: You'll need a large sheet of craft paper and markers.

description: Have kids work together to write a short story by having each write a sentence, one at a time, on a large sheet of craft paper. Give kids the following instructions for their writing:

- **The story must be exciting and full of adventure.**
- **The story must have lots of characters.**
- **The story must reflect the actual interests and abilities of group members.**
- **The story must not have an ending.**

Have kids brainstorm a starting sentence for the story, and write that on the paper. Then form trios, and have trio members work together on the three sentences they'll contribute to the story. Allow one trio at a time to write its additions to the story on the paper. When everyone has finished, have volunteers read the story aloud. Allow kids to continue to add new sentences during upcoming meetings. After a few months, you'll have a unique and fascinating chronicle of the group and its adventures—with a little bit of fantasy and exaggeration thrown in for fun.

Personality Charades

preparation: Before the meeting, prepare several index cards with situations written on them that one person can act out. Possible situations may include "finding out that you failed a test," "reacting to a strange-looking visitor who comes to a youth group meeting," "getting ready for a football game," or "waking up late for school." Prepare one note card for each person.

description: Tell kids that they're going to be playing a variation of Charades. Pass out the note cards, and ask kids not to reveal their situations to anyone else. Say: **Secretly choose another person from the group to portray in the situation on your note card. Act out your situation until someone guesses who you're portraying. Be kind in your portrayals, and don't focus on any negative or inappropriate behaviors.**

After someone guesses correctly, have the person who was portrayed act out his or her situation, portraying another group member. Tell kids that they may not portray anyone more than once. Continue until all kids have been portrayed.

This activity will help kids see the similarities and differences among group members.

personalized Plates

preparation: You'll need plain plastic plates and permanent markers.

description: Give each person a plate and a few markers. Say: **Draw a circle on your plate about two inches from the edge. Write your name in the middle, and decorate the area inside the circle to make the plate your own.**

Once the decorations are complete, allow the plates to dry. Then say: **Now think of one positive word to describe each person in the room, and write that word along the edge of his or her plate. Ready? Go!**

Tell kids it's OK if two people write the same word on one person's plate but to try to keep the words as varied as possible.

When everyone is finished, allow the plates to dry. Read aloud 1 Corinthians 12:12-27, then have pairs discuss these questions:

■ **What's your reaction to the things that people wrote on your plate?**

■ **How do you feel, knowing that your plate is different from everyone else's?**

■ **How can each of us be more accepting of people who are different from us?**

Collect the plates, and keep them at the church. Then take them on retreats or lock-ins for kids to use whenever they eat together as a group.

Person-to-Person Appreciation Prayer

preparation: No preparation is needed for this activity.

description: Form a circle, and have kids grasp hands. Explain that each person will be thanking God for the person on his or her right by thinking of one word that positively describes that person, or one word that tells why he or she appreciates that person. After you've gone around the circle once, have kids break the circle and quickly form a new one, with everyone standing next to at least one new person. Repeat this three or four times. Then close the prayer by having everyone say in unison, "Thank you, God, for (name of the person on the right)."

the Phone Book

preparation: You'll need a few large phone books or thick catalogs (the thicker they are, the better).

description: Have a volunteer come to the front of the room. Hold up a phone book, and say: **You have 30 seconds to tear this book in half.** Start timing immediately—don't give the volunteer any time to think about how to do this. When the time expires, have the kids discuss why this was a difficult, if not impossible, task.

Then have kids stand near the volunteer. Give him or her another book, and say: **Working with other group members, try to tear the book in half in 30 seconds or less.**

If you have more than 10 kids, have groups of about six work on separate books. Give groups a minute to devise their own systems for book tearing. Then give them 30 seconds to make their attempts.

After the tearing, have kids discuss how this task was easier or more difficult with the help of the group. Discuss how this is like or unlike the way kids in the group can help each other.

Phone Book Business Matchups

preparation: You'll need markers and a few old phone books.

description: Form groups of six or fewer, making sure there are an even number of groups. Give each group a marker and an old phone book. Assign each group one of the other groups as a "target" group. Then say: **Go through the Yellow Pages and for each person in your target group find a business that you think describes that person. Make sure all of your choices are positive and reflect the best qualities in each person. When you're finished, you'll share your choices with the whole group.**

Have group members work together to match up businesses with the kids in their target groups. When everyone is finished, have groups take turns presenting their choices. After all of the "matchups" have been shared, have kids tell whether they think their assigned businesses really describe them and explain why or why not. Allow kids who don't think their assigned businesses describe them to choose different businesses.

Congratulate kids on their positive creativity, then have kids mark the businesses they chose, tear out the marked pages, and write the appropriate person's name on each page. Post the pages on a wall of the meeting room for a few weeks.

potato Towers

preparation: You'll need potatoes, toothpicks, and water-based markers.

description: Give each person a potato and a few water-based markers. Say: **If your head were a potato, what would it look like? Re-create your head on your potato.**

When kids are finished, have them display their potatoes for the group. Then distribute toothpicks, and say: **Now work together to create a giant, free-standing potato-head tower.**

When the tower is finished, say: **Wow! It's amazing what you can accomplish when you all put your heads together.**

Ask:

■ **How is this tower like our group?**
■ **What might the toothpicks represent?**
■ **How could we make this tower stronger?**
■ **How can we make our group stronger?**

Have kids take their potatoes home, wash them, and eat them sometime during the upcoming week.

praying Through the Paper

preparation: You'll need the world and local news sections from several days' newspapers.

description: Form groups of three to five. Give each group a newspaper section, and ask kids to search for stories of tragedy and pain. Have each group choose one story or situation that is of particular concern to the kids in the group. After they've chosen stories, have groups discuss the following questions:

- **What are the people who are affected by this going through?**
- **How would you feel if you were in this situation?**
- **What tough things have you had to deal with in your life? How did you cope with them?**

Say: **One way we can reach out to others as a group is through prayer. In your small group, pray for the people who are affected by this tragedy.**

After groups have prayed, bring everyone together to pray again, with each group contributing something about the group's specific situation to the prayer.

After your prayer time, encourage kids to meet together once a week (maybe before school) to pray for people going through difficult times. Kids will soon discover that praying together helps to create solid bonds of friendship and to strengthen the whole group.

remote Control

preparation: You'll need a remote control (an old, broken one is fine), pencils, and copies of the "My Personal Remote" handout (p. 113).

description: Form a circle, and have kids toss around a remote control. Each time someone catches the remote, have that person share one aspect of life he or she would like to have more control over. For example, someone might say, "I wish I could keep my parents from fighting" or "I wish I could have a consistent quiet time."

After everyone has shared once or twice, set the remote in the center of the circle, and distribute the "My Personal Remote" handouts and pencils. Have kids complete the handout then share it with a partner. Have partners pray together, asking God to help them give him absolute "remote control" over their lives.

rolled-Up Record

preparation: You'll need markers and a 50-foot roll of paper.

description: At the beginning or end of a meeting or event, pull out the roll of paper, and have each person write something on it pertinent to the meeting or event. For example, kids might write what they hope to get out of a certain meeting topic, list ways the event helped them, or identify prayer concerns. Unroll the paper enough for each person to write at the same time. Mark off the section, date it, and put the roll away. Every week (or once or twice a month if you'd prefer), get out the roll and repeat the process. Continue doing this until kids have filled the entire roll with notes.

Periodically, have volunteers read aloud the entries on the roll of paper. You may discover ideas that can help you build the group or issues that require more discussion and prayer.

my Personal Remote

If you had a magical remote control device with which you could control all of the difficult areas of your life, what would it look like? Complete the remote control device here by labeling the buttons to reflect areas of your life that you wish you had more control over. Then share your personal remote with a friend.

Scavenger Giveaway

preparation: You'll need vehicles and insured, reliable drivers. Supplies needed will depend on kids' choices of giveaway items.

description: Have kids form groups of no more than four. Make sure each group has a vehicle and a driver. Then tell groups to choose an item to give away to strangers. The item should be appealing while serving to identify the group. For example, a group might decide to give away cookies decorated with phrases or words that describe the youth group. Another group might want to give away mementos of previous group events (with your permission, of course). When groups have determined what items to give away, help them to collect or create their items. Then have kids complete a "reverse scavenger hunt," going house to house and giving their items away.

After this reverse scavenger hunt, have kids form groups of no more than four and discuss the following questions:

■ **How did people respond when you wanted to give them something?**

■ **How is that like the way people react when you try to tell them about your faith? How is it different?**

■ **How can our identity as a group help us to reach out to others?**

Searchlight

preparation: You'll need to meet in a room that can be darkened. You'll also need a flashlight.

description: Have kids sit in a circle on the floor. Darken the meeting room so kids can't see each other. Have a volunteer become the Searcher and stand in the center of the circle with a flashlight. Instruct the group members to take turns calling out things people do to hurt each other or God. For example, kids might say, "Tell a lie," "Swear," or "Cheat at school." Have the Searcher attempt to shine the flashlight on the person speaking before he or she stops talking.

If the Searcher shines the light on someone before he or she finishes speaking, then that person must move to the center of the circle and become the new Searcher.

Continue until several kids have had a chance to be the Searcher. Then turn on the lights, and have kids form pairs to discuss these questions:

- **What's your reaction to this activity?**
- **How is the Searcher like or unlike the Holy Spirit?**

Read aloud James 5:16. Say: **Just as we tried to avoid the light during this activity, we often try to avoid admitting our sins. But God wants us to admit our sins so that we can find peace.**

Have pairs pray together, asking God to help them know how to confess their sins to one another and thanking God for his forgiveness.

Step Inside the Banner

preparation: You'll need several colors of fluorescent paint, paintbrushes, a refrigerator box, and a black light (mounted on a 4-foot board). Cut away the top and bottom of the refrigerator box. Then cut a doorway (or flap) into one side of the box that is big enough for kids to enter the box.

description: As teenagers arrive, give them paintbrushes and fluorescent paint. Have them go into the box one at a time and decorate the inside like a banner that describes your group. Have kids use words, symbols, or drawings—anything that illustrates your group.

When each person has added to the banner box, place the black light over the top of the box and turn it on. Turn off other lights in the room and have kids enter the banner box one at a time to view the finished project. You may want to leave the banner box in the room so kids may add to it during coming weeks. Or you may want to set the banner box up in the church foyer for other church members to visit and view.

tangled Up

preparation: You'll need a 20-foot length of yarn for every two people in your group. All the yarn should be the same color.

description: Send one-third of your group members out of the room. Form pairs among the remaining group members, and give each pair a 20-foot length of yarn. Have partners each tie one end of the yarn to one of their wrists so that pairs are connected by the yarn. Then have kids mingle until they're hopelessly tangled up with other group members.

Then bring the rest of the group members back into the room, and have them guess who's tied to whom, without any help from the kids who are connected by the yarn. After kids figure out who's connected, have them attempt to untangle the tied-up group members. Time the untangling, and then repeat the activity with each of the other two thirds of the class taking a turn leaving the room.

Tip: *This activity is a great companion to a meeting about helping one another with problems, working together, or examining how we're all connected through Christ.* ∎

teenager of the Week

preparation: No preparation is needed for this activity.

description: This identity-builder can be used each week to help kids get to know each other better. Have one group member stand in front of the group as you interview that person about his or her hobbies, interests, dreams, and dislikes. Instruct kids that if the teenager being interviewed mentions something that's also true of one of them, that person is to stand and say, "Me too!" Over the course of a few months, your kids will discover what they share with each other and may develop stronger friendships.

thanks, "Teach"

preparation: You'll need a variety of supplies such as balloons, pipe cleaners, colored paper, dowels, twigs, colored paper clips, masking tape, and any other craft items you can find.

description: Place all of the art supplies on a table, and have kids choose an item that best represents how they feel about a specific teacher they've learned a lot from (such as a schoolteacher, a Sunday school teacher, or a youth group leader). Then have each person explain the item he or she chose. For example, someone might choose a paper clip and say, "I chose a paper clip because our youth group leader holds us together when we need to stay close."

Then have kids use the supplies to create small sculptures representing what they appreciate most about their chosen teachers. Have kids tell what the sculptures represent; then place the sculptures in the middle of the room, and form a circle around them.

Ask:

■ **What can we learn about each other by looking at these sculptures?**

■ **What do these sculptures tell us about the qualities of a good teacher?**

■ **What teaching qualities do the members of our own group have?**

■ **How can we use these qualities to make our group better?**

this Is Our Movie

preparation: No preparation is necessary.

description: Form trios, and have the kids in each trio discuss what kind of a movie might be made to depict the life of your group and why. For example, kids might say, "A western, because people are always getting 'shot down' " or "A science fiction movie, because no one would ever believe this group is real."

Have trios tell the whole group the type of movie they chose and why. Then have trios "cast" their movie by assigning real actors to play the members of their trio in the movie. Remind kids to be kind and flattering in their choices and to choose people who reflect a positive aspect of the trio members they'd be playing. For example, someone might say, "John would be played by Harrison Ford because he's always so cool in the face of danger."

After trios share their casting ideas with the whole group, ask:

■ **How is our group like a drama? a western? a love story? a science fiction movie? a horror film? a documentary?**

■ **What good things would a reviewer have to say about a movie based on the true happenings in this group? What would he or she say could be improved?**

this Is Our Song

preparation: You'll need a CD player, a cassette recorder, and a blank cassette. Invite kids ahead of time to bring in a favorite cassette or CD. Encourage kids to choose songs that have lyrics that are compatible with Christianity. Have a few contemporary

Christian cassettes or CDs available for kids to listen to as well.

description: When kids arrive, have them each tell about a favorite song and play a short part of it. Then have kids work together to choose words from each song that could be put together to say something about your whole group. For example, kids might piece together parts of songs so they say, "We care for each other, and we want to know more about Jesus."

Consider having extra cassettes, cassette players, and CD players available and doing this activity in groups of about six. Have small groups put their finished projects together to form one complete song that describes the group.

This activity may take 15 to 30 minutes, as kids must first listen to songs, decide what they want to say, and finally record the song parts in proper order onto a blank cassette. Have kids review the printed lyrics on cassette or CD sleeves to speed up the process. Allow kids to insert their own words between song parts if they can't find all of the words or phrases they want. Play your group song periodically to remind kids of what the group is all about.

tomorrow's History Lesson

preparation: You'll need a video camera, a VCR, a TV, and clothes that older people might wear. If it's available, theatrical makeup will add to the fun.

description: Have kids discuss what youth ministry might be like in 60 years. Then have kids dress up in old clothes and make themselves up to look 60 years older.

Say: **Imagine that 60 years have passed and you're making a video to tell about the past 60 years of youth ministry. Record one another telling stories about how youth ministry has changed over the years, focusing on what kids used to do for fun, what they did in youth meetings, and what kinds of special events they attended.**

Have kids take turns running the camera and telling stories. Then play back the videotape for all to enjoy.

After the group has viewed the videotape, ask:

■ **What things do you think will stay the same in youth ministry in the future?**

■ **What things about our group are fads that will likely change?**

■ **What things about our group are lasting and might be reflected in future groups?**

top-Secret Files

preparation: You'll need file folders, paper, pens, and markers.

description: Give kids each a blank file-folder and a few markers. Have kids write their names on their folders and decorate their folders to reflect their personalities. When everyone is finished, form groups of four, and have kids explain their folders to their groups.

Give each person a sheet of paper. Have kids write the date on their papers and place them in their folders. Say: **These folders will** become our new, "top-secret" caring files. I'll keep them here in the meeting room so any time you want, you can write someone a positive note, ask for prayer, or share a favorite Bible passage. Let's start filling these files by writing something positive about each person in the room.

Distribute pens, and have each group member write a positive note in each other group member's folder. Then file the folders in a box or file cabinet, and keep it in the room.

For the next several weeks, encourage kids to use the files to express love and build relationships with others in the group.

trading Cards

preparation: You'll need to collect pictures of your group members. Collect copies of their school pictures; take pictures yourself, or have one of your kids take them; or choose pictures from group events that clearly show group members' faces. You'll also need 5x7 index cards cut in half (to make 3½x5-inch cards), glue sticks, and pens.

description: Give each person a picture of another group member and a 3½x5-inch card. Have kids use glue sticks to attach the photos to one side of the cards. Then ask kids to come up with positive "statistics" for their pictured group members in the following categories:

■ best school subjects
■ favorite hobbies and interests
■ positive qualities this person adds to the group

Tell kids they may discuss the statistics with any group members except the one pictured on the card. Have kids write the statistics on the back of the person's card.

When the cards are finished, have kids share them with the group. Have other group members suggest and make changes that would make each card more accurate.

A local printer can make copies on card stock or just make halftones of the photos so that they'll duplicate better. Then you can use a photocopier and heavy paper stock to print the cards. You may want to give your group members copies of a different person's card each week. Advertise this feature by telling kids to "Come every week, and collect the whole set." Be sure to have kids create cards for new group members, too.

truth Belts

preparation: You'll need heavy-duty aluminum foil, tape, and permanent markers.

description: Form pairs, and give each person a 6-foot length of aluminum foil, tape, and a permanent marker. Have partners wrap the foil—without folding or crumpling it—around each other's torsos to create wide "truth belts," securing them with tape. Then ask kids to use permanent markers to write positive "truths" about the other group members on their truth belts. For example, someone might write, "You have a fun way of looking at life" or "You respect other people."

When everyone is finished, have kids return to their pairs to discuss these questions:

■ **What's one thing that was written on your truth belt that you didn't expect to see?**

■ **What does this activity tell us about our group as a whole?**

Vacation Island

preparation: You'll need a world map, a stamp pad, and any rubber stamp. Attach the world map to a wall in your room.

description: Tell kids that they're going to be tour guides and they will be able to take the group anywhere in the world.

Have the first tour guide come up to the map, use the stamp to mark the location to which he or she wants to take the group, and explain why it would be a good vacation spot. Then have the other kids share reasons they would or wouldn't want to go to that location. Allow three or four responses. Then have the tour guide hand the stamp and stamp pad to someone else. When everyone has been a tour guide, ask kids to share what it was like to choose a vacation for the whole group.

Voices From the Other Side

preparation: You'll need one Bible for each person.

description: Form pairs, and give each person a Bible. Have kids face their partners and hold their Bibles up in front of their faces so they can't see each other. Say: **While remaining in this position, share your answer to this question with your partner, "What do you want out of life?"**

Give pairs about two minutes to answer the question. While kids are sharing, make sure they keep their Bibles in front of their faces. After two minutes, have pairs discuss these questions:

■ **What's your reaction to talking from behind your Bible?**

■ **Was it easier or more difficult to share with your partner this way? Explain.**

■ **How is this like the way we put up barriers between ourselves and non-Christians?**

■ **How can we avoid putting up barriers between ourselves and others in this group?**

Have kids read Colossians 3:12-17, and ask:

■ **How can obeying this passage help us draw closer together within this group?**

Webbed Together

preparation: You'll need a skein of yarn.

description: Have kids scatter and sit on the floor. Give one person a skein of yarn, and have him or her wrap the yarn around his or her waist a couple of times then pass it on to someone else to do the same. Continue until the entire group has been tightly "webbed" together, making sure all of the connections are taut.

When the web is complete, point out two people in the center of the group, and say to them: **Let's pretend that this whole group has gotten wrapped up in sin. Group members don't live for God, they just come to church and pretend to live a godly life. They don't really know the first thing about Jesus or real Christian faith. Now imagine that you don't want to be like the group, so you're going to take a stand. You're going to be different, to stand out, to rise above the crowd. So stand up, and be different.**

When the two kids stand, others in the group will be affected and may have to move. That's OK. Once the kids are standing, have the whole group discuss these questions:

■ **What happened when these two stood up?**

■ **How is that like what happens to this group in real life when one or more of you deepen your commitment to God?**

■ **Do your choices really affect the people around you? Why or why not?**

Have everyone in the group stand and pull the yarn tight, then have one person try to sit down. Ask:

■ **If we're all standing up for Christ, how does our combined strength help when one of us is tempted to fall down?**

■ **What does this experience tell you about how each of us can affect the group?**

We Can Do That . . .

preparation: No preparation is needed for this activity.

description: Form a circle, then say: **We each bring unique gifts and abilities to this group. And together we can do great things. Let's see just what kinds of great things we could do.**

Have kids brainstorm outrageous challenges that they might attempt to accomplish, even if they never actually would. Here are a few ideas to get things started:

- build a house,
- cross the ocean,
- design a new line of clothes,
- climb Mount Everest, or
- move the entire church building across the street.

After kids have come up with several ideas, have them choose two or three and determine how each group member could contribute to the completion of the event. For example, someone might suggest that Tom could help design the house because he's a good artist or that Nan could help pour the concrete because she's good at making things smooth or that Tyra could help keep the project on track because she's so good at keeping things organized.

Make sure that each person is given (or comes up with) a way to help accomplish the outrageous task. Then close the activity by affirming the wonderful things the group can do simply by supporting one another in love and reaching out into the community with that same love.

We're Not . . .

preparation: You'll need craft paper, markers, and tape.

description: This is a fun way to help kids discover what makes their group unique and strong.

Tape a huge sheet of craft paper on a wall (or even around the entire room). Then have someone write in giant letters, "Our youth group is not . . ." across the banner. Give kids markers, and have them list thoughts to complete the sentence. Kids might add things such as " . . . an exclusive club" or " . . . quick to judge others." Encourage kids to be honest but kind.

When the banner is packed with ideas, have kids read them all. Ask kids to tell what this banner suggests about the group. Then close by asking God to help the group be the best it can be according to God's design.

What Does It Mean?

preparation: You'll need paper and pencils.

description: Form pairs. Have partners work together to create a new word that reflects a positive aspect of the youth group. The words can be as plain or as funny-sounding as kids desire. For example, a pair might come up with the word "lafnotoxic" to mean "able to laugh at just about anything." Tell pairs to write down their words and definitions.

When pairs are ready, distribute more paper, and have one pair read and spell a word. Ask other pairs to write down the word and what they think it means. Collect the papers—including the original one—and read them aloud. Have kids applaud each answer they think might be correct. Then reveal the correct definition, and have other pairs repeat the process.

When all of the definitions have been read, have kids give themselves a standing ovation for being members of such a great group.

Where Are We?

preparation: You'll need sheets of newsprint, tape, and markers.

description: Form groups of no more than four, and have each group brainstorm the characteristics of a healthy and growing group such as a family, a group of friends, or the youth group.

Encourage kids to be realistic but honest about what they think is important for group health. Have groups list their ideas on newsprint, then tape the newsprint sheets onto a wall.

After groups explain their ideas, have kids vote on the characteristics they believe are most important. Cross off those that are less important or not important to the whole group.

Form pairs, and have partners discuss what grade they would give the group on the most important characteristics. Once partners agree on the grades, have pairs share those grades with the whole group. If the grades are lower than you expected or lower than you think they should be, ask how the group can improve its grades. If the grades are high, ask why they're so good.

Have someone make a complete list of the characteristics and post it in the meeting room. Complete a grade checkup twice a year to keep on top of how the kids think the group is doing.

You Can Quote Me

preparation: No preparation is necessary for this activity.

description: Tell kids they're to answer the following questions, using only titles or quotes from popular movies, television shows, children's stories, or songs. For example, someone might answer a question with "I don't think so, Tim" (from *Home Improvement*) or "I think I can . . ." (from the children's book, *The Little Engine That Could*). Ask:

- **What words best describe our group?**
- **What words best describe the strengths of our group?**
- **What words best describe something we can improve in our group?**
- **What words best describe something God might say about our group?**

Create your own questions to make this activity more meaningful to your own group.

Youth Group Logo

preparation: You'll need paper and pens or markers.

description: Form groups of four or five, and have each group think of two characteristics that make the youth group special. As a large group, discuss these characteristics, and choose the top three. Then have kids work together to create a simple logo that represents these characteristics. For example, if one of the characteristics is "We love each other," the logo might include a heart shape. Try to keep the logo simple so that all kids can duplicate it.

Have kids think of ways to use this group logo to remind themselves of who they are as a group. For example, kids might want to create T-shirts using the logo or create a large banner to hang in the room. Make sure kids are prepared to answer questions about what the logo means. Also make sure that kids know that the logo should be a means for inviting others, not excluding them.